About This Book

Why is this topic important?

Organizations are in search of the training solutions that will provide them with the most fast-acting and relevant ways to deal with the needs of their workforce in a constantly and rapidly changing environment. In this search, companies have transitioned from classroom training to e-learning to blended learning in the blink of an eye. Now, training professionals are realizing that classroom training will remain central to training programs, with alternative solutions such as e-learning, mentoring, coaching, and/or job aids providing effective enhancements.

What can you achieve with this book?

This book introduces blended learning where classroom training is the key component and where other training solutions support and supplement what is learned in the classroom. The definitions and explanations of various components of a blended learning solution provide trainers with the resources needed to implement blended learning in any organization.

How is this book organized?

In an easy-to-use format, this practical guide starts with Part 1, containing general information on blended learning and six specific steps for creating a blended learning program. Part 2 of the book contains chapters outlining nine of the most common solutions that make up blended learning and information on how to implement each of them. The resource materials included in each chapter will make it easy for training professionals to put blended learning into practice in their organizations. Finally, Part 3 contains several examples of common classroom training programs converted to blended training programs, along with the steps taken to convert them.

About Pfeiffer

Pfeiffer serves the professional development and hands-on resource needs of training and human resource practitioners and gives them products to do their jobs better. We deliver proven ideas and solutions from experts in HR development and HR management, and we offer effective and customizable tools to improve workplace performance. From novice to seasoned professional, Pfeiffer is the source you can trust to make yourself and your organization more successful.

Essential Knowledge Pfeiffer produces insightful, practical, and comprehensive materials on topics that matter the most to training and HR professionals. Our Essential Knowledge resources translate the expertise of seasoned professionals into practical, how-to guidance on critical workplace issues and problems. These resources are supported by case studies, worksheets, and job aids and are frequently supplemented with CD-ROMs, Web sites, and other means of making the content easier to read, understand, and use.

Essential Tools Pfeiffer's Essential Tools resources save time and expense by offering proven, ready-to-use materials—including exercises, activities, games, instruments, and assessments—for use during a training or team-learning event. These resources are frequently offered in looseleaf or CD-ROM format to facilitate copying and customization of the material.

Pfeiffer also recognizes the remarkable power of new technologies in expanding the reach and effectiveness of training. While e-hype has often created whizbang solutions in search of a problem, we are dedicated to bringing convenience and enhancements to proven training solutions. All our e-tools comply with rigorous functionality standards. The most appropriate technology wrapped around essential content yields the perfect solution for today's on-the-go trainers and human resource professionals.

www.pfeiffer.com *Essential resources for training and HR professionals*

The Other Blended Learning

A Classroom-Centered Approach

DIANN WILSON

ELLEN SMILANICH

Foreword by Mel Silberman

Pfeiffer

A Wiley Imprint
www.pfeiffer.com

ISBN: 0-7879-7401-3

CIP data on file with the Library of Congress.

Acquiring Editor: Martin Delahoussaye   Manufacturing Supervisor: Becky Carreño
Director of Development: Kathleen Dolan Davies   Editorial Assistant: Laura Reizman
Production Editor: Nina Kreiden   Illustrations: Lotus Arts
Editor: Rebecca Taff

Printed in the United States of America

Printing   10 9 8 7 6 5 4 3 2 1

CONTENTS

PART 3

Sample Designs Converting Classroom Training to Blended Learning

FOREWORD

TODAY'S RAPIDLY CHANGING and competitive business environment demands that organizations train their employees effectively. Active training has made great strides in enhancing the effectiveness of classroom training, and now blended learning is extending its contribution to additional training delivery systems.

If you are new to blended learning, *The Other Blended Learning: A Classroom-Centered Approach* has everything you need to get started. If you have already been using blended learning in your organization but want to increase your effectiveness, you'll find that this easy-to-use reference provides a plethora of resources to enhance your existing blended learning efforts.

Since many organizations rely on classroom training as their primary method for educating employees, this book focuses on how to add training methods to classroom training to create a blended learning solution. The authors work from a firm understanding that the purpose of training is to enhance organizational results, and they demonstrate how to use the most appropriate training solutions to impact the bottom line.

In *The Other Blended Learning: A Classroom-Centered Approach,* Diann Wilson and Ellen Smilanich draw on their considerable experience in the private and public sectors and as members of both large and small training departments. Their work is firmly grounded in adult learning and instructional design theory. Having worked in education and in business and as internal trainers and outside consultants, Diann and Ellen are able to provide both the academic and practical aspects of implementing blended learning in your organization.

This practical guide is easy to read and is useful for training professionals, HR professionals, non-trainers who are called on to do training in their organizations, and executives who need to understand the importance of blended learning as an effective training method. The book provides an outline of the blended learning process in addition to an overview of numerous training solutions. For those who want to delve deeper into various solutions, the annotated references direct readers to additional resources.

The first section of the book offers a step-by-step process, which leads you through the steps necessary to design, develop, and evaluate a blended learning program. It contains guides and resources, including a unique decision matrix to help you select which training solutions would be the most effective for your particular situation. Part 2 includes chapters on nine of the more common training solutions that can be "blended" with classroom training. Each of these chapters is organized identically and includes a definition of the solution, when it's most effectively used, its pros and cons, steps for implementation, sample materials, and an annotated bibliography. Part 3 contains before-and-after examples of six situations, where traditional classroom training has been transformed into a blended learning solution. Finally, the authors provide numerous practical examples, tools, and case studies throughout the book that demonstrate how you can enhance your training effectiveness through the use of blended learning.

Enjoy this worthwhile book.

Mel Silberman
President, Active Training

ACKNOWLEDGMENTS

WE WOULD LIKE to give credit to all of the individuals who helped us in writing and publishing our first book. First and foremost, we thank Martin Delahoussaye for his faith in us and the encouragement he provided. Thanks also to Bonnie Burn, whose experience provided both encouragement and wisdom. Elizabeth Pecsi offered freely of her communications expertise. Thanks to Steve and Rob and our family and friends who understood when we were short with them and who consistently reminded us that we could do it. And finally, thank you to Max, Molly, Alex, and Lucy, who provided entertainment and laughter when we needed it.

The Other Blended Learning

DOES THIS SITUATION SEEM FAMILIAR?

Chris Thomas is the manager of logistics and has twenty employees who all need to receive training on a new process for tracking shipments. The process is complex and Chris feels that the employees will need to receive two levels of training: beginning and advanced. As the training manager, you are asked to deliver the training.

The twenty employees are spread over three shifts and include two employees who work in a satellite location that is out of state. Chris has requested that you conduct two classroom training sessions for the employees, and he would like them on consecutive days to minimize travel time and expenses for the employees who work out of state. He feels you can cover the beginning content on the first day of the training and the advanced content on the second day.

As an experienced trainer, you know that it would be best for the learners if they could practice with the basic content before learning the more advanced aspects of the system. Additionally, you are aware that the employees who are coming to class during a time outside of their shifts will need to be paid overtime, which is quite an expense for the organization. You want to explore alternative training delivery methods with Chris, but he has had success with classroom training in the past, so in the spirit of good customer service, you're tempted to provide what he's asking for.

Or how about this situation?

Your company recently adopted new policies restricting the use of company cell phones and Internet access to business use only. The training department decided the best way to provide the mandatory policy training for all two hundred employees was to conduct instructor-led classroom training sessions. One instructor could accommodate forty employees at a time, which minimized the number of classroom sessions that were required. The class consisted predominantly of the distribution and explanation of the policies, as well as the distribution and collection of a sign-off form that would be kept in each employee's file. Due to the small amount of content being covered, the class length was held to two hours. Although it required some prodding on the part of a few departments, the organization was able to reach a 100 percent participation rate.

Therefore, when the company president decided to introduce a new performance review process, she immediately suggested that the training department use a similar model to conduct the training. Five two-hour class sessions were scheduled, and it was expected that the new forms, the feedback process, and any questions could all be addressed in a classroom setting with forty participants.

The training department felt that a subject of this magnitude required much more time than the introduction of a new cell phone and e-mail policy had taken. In addition, the performance review system involved different responsibilities for different positions. Managers had to prepare to conduct the review discussions, employees had to learn about the process from their own perspectives (which included a self-appraisal), and directors were being asked to review salary increase recommendations, all of which required different skills.

The president was anxious to introduce the new process and was under pressure from the board of directors to implement it quickly. Extensive class development time was not available, and training needed to be completed quickly. The training department wanted to be responsive, but they also wanted the training to be effective.

Circumstances like these occur regularly in organizations around the world. Managers tend to ask for classroom training as a solution to a training need simply because classroom training has met needs in the past. However, the world of work has changed a great deal in the last thirty years and, with it, the world of training. Companies have grown both larger and leaner, more geographically diverse, crossing many time zones as well as encompassing a variety of cultures, countries, and languages. The traditional classroom training model wasn't designed to handle these factors and can't meet all of the learning needs of every individual in every organization.

In today's organizations, training departments are being called on to train people faster, in more locations, and with shorter notice and fewer resources. The evolution of business has caused an evolution in training toward a solution called "blended learning," providing an exciting opportunity for those in the field of training and development. Originally used to describe e-learning combined with additional training solutions, the "other" blended learning has classroom training at its core. In our view of blended learning, training departments have many options in addition to e-learning or classroom training; in fact, blended learning encourages us to look beyond the training department and to use all of an organization's resources to meet the training needs. Because the purpose of any training should be to meet a business need, we offer this definition: *Blended learning is the use of the most effective training solutions, applied in a coordinated manner, to achieve learning objectives that will attain the desired business goals.*

While not necessarily faster or cheaper in the short term, a blended learning program can involve some cost and time savings solutions in the long term and, more importantly, can increase training effectiveness. That, after all, is what training professionals strive for. In this book, we will address increasing training effectiveness through the use of a blended learning program.

How This Book Is Organized

Part 1: Blended Program Design Basics

Part 1 focuses on the steps to follow in order to create a blended learning program.

Chapter 1, "Why Blended Learning Now?," outlines the evolution of blended learning and discusses the benefits to using a variety of coordinated training solutions over a single training method.

Chapter 2, "Overview of the Process," is a summary of the six steps to follow in order to implement a blended learning solution in your organization.

Chapters 3 through 8 provide more in-depth information on each of the steps to follow in order to create a blended learning solution.

Step 1. Determine the Need (Chapter 3)

Step 2. Create Goals and Objectives for the Program (Chapter 4)

Step 3. Design the Blended Program (Chapter 5)

Step 4. Create and Coordinate the Individual Training Solutions (Chapter 6)

Step 5. Implement the Blended Program (Chapter 7)

Step 6. Measure the Results of the Program (Chapter 8)

Part 2: Training Solution Options

A blended learning program consists of the effective selection and synchronization of more than one training solution. This section outlines nine of the more frequently used solutions. We assume our readers will have more familiarity with some solutions than with others; however, we provide basic knowledge for all of the solutions to ensure we meet the needs of a wide variety of readers. Each chapter contains information on what the training solution is, the pros and cons of the individual solution, and how to implement it. Additional tools and resources are also provided to help you get started.

- Classroom Training (Chapter 9)
- Subject-Matter Expert Training (Chapter 10)

- Assessment Instruments (Chapter 11)

- Instructor-Led e-Learning (Chapter 12)

- Self-Study e-Learning (Chapter 13)

- Job Aids (Chapter 14)

- Mentoring (Chapter 15)

- Coaching (Chapter 16)

- On-the-Job Training (Chapter 17)

Part 3: Sample Designs Converting Classroom Training to Blended Learning

There are many ways to blend the various learning solutions to create an effective blended program. This section provides samples of training programs that have been converted from a traditional program to a blended learning program by using the steps and tools outlined in this book.

- Sample 1: Business Writing

- Sample 2: Customer Service

- Sample 3: Orientation

- Sample 4: Software Implementation

- Sample 5: Train-the-Trainer

- Sample 6: Management

PART 1

Blended Program Design Basics

In Part 1 of this book we discuss how to create a blended learning program. We offer six steps for creating a blended learning approach, which—being hands-on practitioners ourselves—we realize won't always be the way you'll actually complete the process in the real world. The world of work does not always allow the time or resources needed to complete every step fully and in the appropriate order. We provide the steps for your use as an outline and a guide and trust that you'll take from them what works for you given your time and resources.

1

Why Blended Learning Now?

After nine years with the same organization, Jenna had worked her way up from being a trainer to being the director of training and development. In her years with the company, she had seen a lot of changes. When she started, she and her two training colleagues mostly developed and led classroom-training sessions that ranged in length from two hours to five days, each with basically the same format: presentation of new material followed by some kind of interactive exercise.

In the meantime, the company experienced a growth spurt. The company had grown not just locally, but through the purchase of manufacturing plants and smaller companies. At first, these facilities were concentrated solely in the United States, but eventually new sites overseas were acquired as well. All of this had a significant impact on the training department.

As the company grew, so did the demand for training classes, and other trainers were added to the staff to meet the need. More classroom training sessions were held, and one of the conference rooms had to be converted to a classroom to accommodate the demand. Since the company had become more widespread, this created quite a challenge, as training was now needed for more employees and in more locations.

Along with the continued growth came an increased focus on company productivity. Managers began to demand shorter classes; people were just too busy with their job responsibilities to sit in a classroom, no matter how important the new information was. As the years passed, the demands for even shorter sessions grew, and some managers became reluctant to send their employees to training at all unless it was mandatory.

Because of the drive for lower operating costs, the training budget originally remained stable, but it eventually was reduced. The training staff shrank, and Jenna and her staff found themselves being expected to cover the same amount of material in an increasingly shorter time. As they reduced the length of their classes, they found they were getting less than satisfactory results.

Training delivery had to change, and it did. Since travel budgets were tight, the trainers were not able to be physically available at each of the company's locations, so the various facilities were left to fend for themselves. Supervisors were expected to train any new employees, although many of them had no training expertise. In addition, most supervisors had to provide training on top of performing all of their other regular job responsibilities, which left them with limited time to prepare to train. Sometimes more seasoned employees were asked to train less experienced workers. When new corporate-wide initiatives were introduced, the training department was still held responsible. Due to budget cuts, however, instead of traveling to the various job sites to conduct classroom training, Jenna and her staff often used videoconferences (for those sites that had the equipment), Internet-delivered presentations using WebEx or NetMeeting, or technology-based training programs delivered via the intranet or CD-ROM.

Unfortunately, these alternatives were not always successful. Since the training function was sometimes delegated to those who lacked any training background or education, no formal evaluation was completed, and even the "successes" were measured only through word-of-mouth feedback. Other less-than-positive feedback was received as well. For example, the IT department, which managed the many desktop applications, decided to deliver technical training solely through computer-based training, buying off-the-shelf training products for general application use. These computer-based training modules were state-of-the-art but, as IT soon discovered, quickly became outdated and, after the first few months of implementation, were largely ignored by the users. The intended audience members reported through informal feedback that the programs were boring, were not very applicable, and, in many cases, were simply too difficult to use at the workstations, especially since they had to compete with the employees' ongoing job responsibilities.

Due to the lack of effectiveness of the alternative training solutions, the pendulum eventually began to swing back, and the training department was asked to deliver more classroom training. This time, however, Jenna and her colleagues used the lessons learned from the past, created more effective classroom sessions, and augmented the learning process through a variety of coordinated learning solutions. For example, new employee orientation was delivered primarily as a classroom session, but the participants were also provided work-specific job aids, weekly e-mail reminders, and short discussion sessions scheduled at the participants' one-, three-, and six-month anniversaries. By carefully considering which training solutions would best meet particular training needs, Jenna was able to stay within her budget while effectively providing training to her organization. At the time, she felt that this mix of learning methods was most effective for her organization in a rigid economy. It wasn't until later that she learned that she had successfully implemented blended learning.

What Is Blended Learning?

The fast-paced changes that have occurred in the world of work have had quite an influence on the training profession. While classroom training was originally the typical method of delivering training, the 1990s introduced the use of technology, and many organizations jumped on the e-learning bandwagon. Mixed successes combined with continued workplace changes have led many organizations back to using the classroom as the backbone of their training programs. Despite the popularity of using computers for training, a recent American Society for Training and Development (ASTD) study showed that while there has been an increase in alternative delivery methods, classroom training remains the most popular form of instruction in organizations (Sugrue and Kim, 2004).

However, the key to an effective training program is not to rely solely on any one method, but to use a variety of training solutions instead. No single delivery method is ideal for all types of training, so blended learning was developed to meet the changing needs of organizations. The term *blended learning* was originally used to describe e-learning combined with additional training solutions such as job aids, on-the-job training, or mentoring.

Blended learning generally means the application of two or more methods or solutions to a learning need. However, since the purpose of any training should be to meet a business need, we offer a refined definition:

> Blended learning is the use of the most effective training solutions, applied in a coordinated manner, to achieve learning objectives that will attain the desired business goals.

Due to the widespread use of and knowledge about classroom training, in this book we describe the design and use of the "other" blended learning, which has traditional classroom training as its nucleus, combined with one or more additional training solutions.

Using this model, blended learning can take many forms. Some examples include:

- Conducting a new employee orientation in a classroom led by an instructor, following up with e-mails and electronic checklists that employees must finish in order to complete the orientation process.

- Holding traditional workshops or seminars in conjunction with ongoing e-mail dialogues to answer questions and encourage application of the principles taught in class.

- Providing classroom instruction on new computer software, followed by on-the-job training to demonstrate how the software is specifically used in each learner's department and to ensure application of learning on the job.

- Offering traditional seminars on management skills for new supervisors, with mentoring provided afterward by seasoned managers.

- Teaching basic features of a new application via a computer-based training program, followed by teaching the advanced skills in the classroom.

Many business, government, educational, and service organizations have embraced blended learning. The U.S. Food and Drug Administration (FDA), for example, has initiated a blended learning approach for its auditors and is inviting industry leaders to take part in this new approach to compliance training. A recent study conducted by Balance Learning, in conjunction with *Training* magazine (Blended Learning, 2003) found that:

- Over half of the 173 organizations surveyed in the UK are using blended learning;

- Half of those using blended learning deliver over 50 percent of their training this way; and

- Some organizations spend over three-quarters of their budgets on blended learning approaches.

While many organizations in the United States have been using some form of blended learning, they may not have been referring to it by this term. In the past, handouts, workbooks, or job aids have often accompanied classroom training. However, since the inception of e-learning, the term "blended learning" was coined to refer to the combination of e-learning with traditional methods. The concept has now broadened into a more robust, widely used, and effective solution to organizations' training needs.

Advantages of Blended Learning

No single delivery method is ideal for all types of training; for one thing, different subject matter typically requires different training methods. Blended learning allows the training professional to address learning needs in the manner most appropriate for the business needs being addressed, typically with classroom instruction as the centerpiece. A best-in-class approach to instruction combines the best instructor-led training with the best additional methods of training.

The benefits for you and your organization to using this approach include:

- Widened reach of training;
- Ease of implementation;
- Cost-effectiveness;
- Optimized business results;
- Meeting diverse needs; and
- Improved training responsiveness.

Widened Reach of Training

A single method of training delivery limits the reach of a training program in some manner. A classroom training program, for example, limits access to only those who can participate at the set time and at the geographic location. Offering alternatives to classroom training through other delivery methods allows those who cannot be physically present in the classroom to have access to learning.

Ease of Implementation

Many organizations have already been using some form of blended learning, so implementation could be as simple as ensuring that needs have been assessed and that training has been effectively designed and coordinated to meet those needs. In this situation, no formal rollout of a new program would be required. For organizations that have not experimented with combined training solutions, in this book we outline six steps for implementing blended learning. Chapters 3 through 8 provide the outline for the process; Chapters 9 through 17 describe the particulars for some of the major components of a blended learning program.

Cost-Effectiveness

Blended learning provides options for organizations, allowing them to use the solutions that best meet their organizational needs. When cost is a major consideration, companies can select from those training solutions that are most economical, which will help them manage to a budget.

Optimized Business Results

Organizations can realize exceptional results from blended learning initiatives. In a blended learning best practice survey conducted by the eLearning Guild (2003), 73.6 percent of respondents reported blended learning to be more effective than non-blended approaches. Travel is also minimized by applying additional training methods to the traditional classroom training solution, and reduced travel allows more time for actual work as well as lower travel costs.

Meeting Diverse Needs

Learning style theory proposes that different people learn in different ways; research shows that, while some people prefer to learn by listening, others prefer to read about a concept, and still others need to see a demonstration. Blended learning addresses these different learning styles by providing a variety of learning solutions and methodologies.

Blended learning conducted via the computer (e-learning) can provide training for a geographically diverse workforce, allowing them to participate in training on their own schedule. E-learning solutions also help to meet the needs of an increasingly more technologically savvy workforce. Additionally, adult learners typically prefer to learn by applying the new information to their own experiences, and a classroom-centered blended learning program allows them to do so effectively.

Improved Training Responsiveness

Combining training solutions provides the flexibility organizations need to address the ever-shrinking half-life of knowledge and the need for a faster deployment of information—particularly with a geographically dispersed workforce.

Organizations can choose the solutions that meet their needs and budgets. Learners have various delivery methods to meet their job-responsibility and learning-style needs. This combination yields a learning solution that is both responsive to and effective for all organizations and individuals.

KEY POINTS

- The field of training has changed a great deal in recent years in response to significant changes in the world of work.

- Blended learning is an effective way to meet new business needs.

- Offering a variety of learning solutions can increase the effectiveness of a training program while reducing or controlling costs at the same time.

RESOURCES

Blended learning: The here and now. (2003, November). *Training.*
eLearning Guild. (2003, February). *The blended learning best practices survey.*
Sugrue, B., & Kim, K. (2004). *ASTD state of the industry report.* Alexandria, VA: ASTD.

2

Overview of the Process

PRECISELY HOW YOU WILL IMPLEMENT a blended learning program in your organization is dependent on the characteristics of your business. An international bank with 1,500 employees and a ten-person training department would take a very different approach than would a public agency with three hundred employees and one trainer. An organization that has already been using multiple training solutions may be able to implement a coordinated blended learning program more easily than would one that has been relying only on classroom training. Whatever your situation, the six steps outlined below provide the foundation for effectively implementing blended learning.

Some of the steps in designing and implementing a blended training program are similar to designing and implementing *any* training solution, and these may be steps you are already taking. For example, to be most effective, you must conduct a needs analysis, determine the gap between what is and what should be, and relate the needs back to the business's goals. At the same time, designing and implementing a blended approach differs because you are considering multiple solutions and how they fit together. Each of the steps listed below is described briefly in this chapter and discussed in further detail in Chapters 3 through 8:

1. Determine the need.
2. Create goals and objectives for the program.
3. Design the blended program.
4. Create and coordinate the individual training solutions.
5. Implement the blended program.
6. Measure the results of the program.

1. Determine the Need

Before designing a solution to a problem, you need to know what exactly the problem is. This is also true when implementing a blended learning solution. An assessment of the training need and the information gathered about the learners will provide a solid foundation for your blended program. Unfortunately, this step is often cut short or—worse yet—completely omitted in the training development process, resulting in training that doesn't meet either the perceived or real business needs. It's rather like building a new house without asking the owners what features they need and expecting that somehow the house will meet their expectations. Since many resources already exist that more thoroughly explore the topic of needs assessment, we provide only an overview of the topic in Chapter 3 and a list of resources for additional information.

2. Create Goals and Objectives for the Program

Once the needs have been identified, determine what you intend to achieve with your blended learning program. Clearly identify the goal of the training solution (how it will meet the business need) as well as identify very specific learning outcomes. When a new house is being designed, the architect determines and verifies the expectations, budget, and desires of the owners. From this information, he or she knows very clearly what style, size, and features will meet the owners' expectations, and thus can plan accordingly. Chapter 4 provides instructions on how to record and substantiate the overall goal(s) of a blended learning program as well as why and how to write the specific learning objectives that will attain the goal(s) and resolve the business issue.

3. Design the Blended Program

The learning objectives will lead you to the overall design of your program. The construction of a house would require a blueprint of the entire structure and a project plan that outlines the implementation steps, budget, and timeline of all of the specific components. Chapter 5 provides the following aids to help you with your design: (1) a basic definition of each of the training solutions; (2) a list and descriptions of factors to consider in selecting your training solutions; (3) a matrix that includes both solutions and factors, with guidance as to which solutions will be most effective for your situation; and (4) a template to help you outline your training program.

4. Create and Coordinate the Individual Training Solutions

You would design the specific components of your blended learning program much the same way as the architect would in our house analogy. Different people or teams may design the different solutions, just as electricians, plumbers, and builders design the various elements of a new house. Everyone's designs must be coordinated, just as your individual learning solutions will be in order to meet the identified business goal. We discuss the coordination of this process in Chapter 6.

5. Implement the Blended Program

Finally, the house is actually built. The blueprint is completed, just as all of your individual training components have been designed and developed. The implementation has to be coordinated, just as the design of the house was, which we discuss in Chapter 7.

6. Measure the Results of the Program

Since a blended learning program is intended to help achieve a business need, it is important to measure to what extent that need was met, just as the house owners will conduct a walkthrough of their new house after construction has been completed to be sure everything is as they desired. The various means to evaluate training programs are outlined in Chapter 8.

Pitfalls to Avoid

As with most learning solutions, these steps are intended to provide an optimal design and implementation. However, the world of work does not always allow the time or resources needed to complete every step fully and in the appropriate order. While we acknowledge that you can indeed implement a blended learning program with a few shortcuts, you should take care to avoid some of the more common pitfalls. These include:

- *Starting too big.* If you have been relying solely on classroom training in your organization, do not add e-learning, job aids, mentoring, coaching, and assessment instruments in your first blended program. Start small, experiment, learn from your experience, and build on your program once you have the confidence of the organization.

- *Relying solely on old standbys.* Remember that a blended learning program is a solution to a business problem. Just because you have always used computer-based training does not mean that it is the most effective solution for the business need you uncover. If you and your organization have confidence in one particular learning solution, you may want to stick with it; but be sure to explore all of the factors uncovered in your needs assessment and choose appropriate additional learning solutions as well.

- *Failing to involve senior management.* Launching a new learning program without executive support is like building a house without the homeowners' involvement. Your blended learning program is solving senior management's business need, and they must be aware of what you are doing and how it will help them.

- *Losing focus on the business need.* Some blended programs come with lots of bells and whistles. The more solutions you add and the more clever you become with transitioning from one solution to the next, the easier it is to lose sight of why you were building a blended solution in the first place. Be sure to select, create, and coordinate only those solutions that will meet your business need.

KEY POINTS

- The implementation of blended learning will vary, based on organizational characteristics.

- The six-step process will assist you in designing and developing your blended learning program.

- Preparation can help you avoid common pitfalls in implementing blended learning solutions.

3

Determine the Need

HUMAN RESOURCE PROFESSIONALS are often asked to
provide training for employees. While it's tempting to quickly respond
with a training class, a better response is to first investigate—to confirm that
training will indeed solve the problem and address a business need. Requests
for training are often triggered by *symptoms* of a problem that has arisen. Until
the problem is understood in greater detail, implementing a solution or an
intervention can be costly and ineffective. Unfortunately, HR professionals
often overlook a training needs assessment.

It is important to understand that a *need* is not a want or desire, but a gap
between "what is" and "what should be." The needs assessment serves (1) to
identify the gaps; (2) to consider to what extent the problem can be solved
by training; and (3) to investigate what type of training to offer. Because so
many resources exist that thoroughly explore the topic of needs assessment,
in this chapter we provide only an overview of the topic, some samples, and
a list of resources for additional information.

Why Conduct Needs Assessments?

A needs assessment serves many purposes, including:

- Finding out what knowledge or skills employees need in order to do their jobs;

- Determining whether training will provide the required knowledge or skills; and

- Distinguishing training needs from other organizational problems or issues.

The primary reasons for investigating needs are to ensure that there is an appropriate call for training and to identify the nature of the content. A secondary use of a needs assessment is to gather information about the learners and their attributes, which influences one's choice of training solutions.

How to Assess Needs

Data can be obtained through a variety of techniques. The most common method of assessing needs is through a survey. However, one can also investigate needs through interviews, observations, reviews of existing data, tests, or performance evaluations.

Needs Assessment Surveys

A survey can provide both qualitative and quantitative data and can be distributed to managers or employees to determine needs. If management support is required to ensure that training programs are well-attended, have the managers complete a needs assessment survey. When the results and subsequent feedback are used to determine training content, the managers will know that their input helped shape the training program and will tend to take more ownership of the results. Surveys can be given directly to employees as well by asking them to identify their training needs. Survey questions must be carefully worded to ensure that needs rather than wants are being identified. (See Exhibits 3.1 and 3.2 at the end of this chapter.)

Interviews

A problem analysis interview can also be used to assess training needs. One way to accomplish this is to meet with the department manager and ask open-ended questions to understand the current situation as well as to determine what the manager believes should be happening. Keep in mind that we are conditioned to ask questions about things that aren't working well (the problems) so that we can fix them. Try to also find out about the successes: What *has* worked? For example, interviewing employees who have been accident-free could provide valuable information on how to use training to reduce accidents among employees with a high incidence of accidents. Talking with employees directly can also provide clues to their learning styles, which will help in the design and delivery of your training program. (See Exhibit 3.3 for a sample interview form.)

Observation

Observing exemplary employees can provide insight on how to perform training on tasks efficiently and effectively. Watch how these employees perform their work and what steps or processes they follow, and then construct step-by-step training or develop job aids for less successful employees to use to improve their performance. Additionally, observing employees performing work in their actual setting can help you to develop training that closely simulates the work setting, which will increase the likelihood that learning will result in behavioral change.

Subject-matter experts (SMEs) can also be of great assistance in observing processes, procedures, methods, and practices. For example, you might bring in a SME to perform a safety assessment of the plant operations and a task analysis of the work being performed on the line. The data gathered through this method can be used to construct classroom training, on-the-job training, or job aids, for example.

Review of Existing Data

A variety of production data already exists within organizations, and much of it can be useful in determining training needs. Operational data such as number of products produced, the time required to produce products, or the error rate in production can help pinpoint both what training is needed and which employees need that training.

In addition to production data, many companies are now focusing on competency development, where they determine which core competencies are needed by their employees in order to meet or exceed performance requirements and organizational goals. An assessment of employees against these competencies can provide information about which employees need what training. In turn, some companies are using 360-degree feedback (see Chapter 11, "Assessment Instruments," for more information). The results of these assessments may also play a key part in determining training needs.

Tests

Tests and assessment centers can be used to assess skills, aptitudes, and behaviors for specific jobs. Organizations using these means receive objective feedback about which employees currently possess certain characteristics and about which developmental areas are necessary for certain career paths. For example, some of the typical factors assessed for managerial-level candidates include the ability to set goals, prepare budgets, give employee feedback, and develop teamwork.

Performance Evaluations

Finally, data can be obtained through performance evaluations, which typically indicate areas in which employees must improve to do their jobs effectively. By looking at this data, a trainer can identify training needs and determine how extensive those needs are. Additionally, information on the number of employees with each deficiency and their locations will help you determine which training solution will work best. In addition to a traditional manager-conducted performance review, many companies are turning to performance feedback instruments to gain additional input from peers or customers. From this type of evaluation, companies can decide what programs to use and can track and evaluate the effectiveness of those programs.

How to Analyze Needs

The terms *needs assessment* and *needs analysis* are often used interchangeably. There is, however, a distinction: A needs assessment involves only gathering the information. Then you must *analyze* it to confirm what the training need is and to ensure that there is a tie to a business need.

For example, if you receive a request for customer service training, the need can be assessed by looking at customer service survey data or by observing customer service employees on the job. This assessment will quickly confirm whether there is indeed a gap between what is and what should be. An analysis of this information in conjunction with data about declining sales numbers or repeat customers would reveal the tie to a real business need.

On the other hand, if you complete a needs assessment in response to a request for team-building training, it may not reveal a *need* for such training. In this case, even though there is a *desire* for training, there may be no tie to a business need.

Care should be given to understand the original request for training and to communicate to your "customer" that additional data must be gathered in order to fully understand the problem. A needs assessment will also provide information about which employees require the training and will offer help in determining the most feasible training solutions.

KEY POINTS

- Needs assessments are an important step in confirming a training need and identifying the real problem.
- A variety of methods for conducting needs assessments exist.
- One must analyze the data collected and ensure that a tie to the organization's business needs exists.

RESOURCES

Bartram, S., & Gibson, B. (2000). *The training needs analysis toolkit.* Amherst,
MA: HRD Press. This manual includes techniques for transforming data into
realistic training strategies and solutions and includes twenty-two reproducible
instruments and surveys for gathering information.

Gupta, K. (1998). *A practical guide to needs assessment.* San Francisco, CA: Pfeiffer.
This how-to handbook includes a methodical approach, along with worksheets,
ready-to-use forms, and templates to use when assessing training needs.

McConnell, J. H. (2003). *How to identify your organization's training needs:
A practical guide to needs analysis.* New York: American Management Associa-
tion. This book includes information and step-by-step instructions for determining the training needs of both an organization and its employees. Includes
reproducible forms, checklists, formulas, and interviewing guidelines.

Robinson, D. G., & Robinson, J. C. (1989). *Training for impact: How to link
training to business needs and measure the results.* San Francisco, CA: Pfeiffer.
This hands-on guide presents a twelve-step approach that directly links training to specific organizational goals.

Exhibit 3.1. Sample Needs Assessment Survey for Managers.

Instructions: Please complete this form and return to Human Resources to help us determine how to best meet your training needs.

I Know How to . . .	Yes	Need to learn
Hire the right person for the right job	☐	☐
Orient a new employee to my company	☐	☐
Set and communicate performance expectations to employees	☐	☐
Coach employees to high performance	☐	☐
Document performance discussions	☐	☐
Discuss a performance review	☐	☐
Modify my communication style to the listener	☐	☐
Use different leadership styles depending on the situation	☐	☐
Use a problem-solving method	☐	☐
Make the right decisions	☐	☐
Organize my inbox and complete my work in a timely manner	☐	☐
Write effective business memos, e-mail, and correspondence	☐	☐
Conduct on-the-job training for employees	☐	☐
Prevent sexual harassment in our workplace	☐	☐
Apply local, state, and federal employment laws as I make management decisions	☐	☐

Exhibit 3.2. Sample Needs Assessment Survey for Directors.

Instructions: In order to help us determine our management training needs, please assess each of your manager's ability to carry out the following responsibilities on a scale of 1 to 4, with 1 being poor and 4 being excellent:

As a manager, he or she is able to:

Develop plans	1	2	3	4
Successfully carry out plans	1	2	3	4
Manage change effectively	1	2	3	4
Motivate employees	1	2	3	4
Manage employee performance	1	2	3	4
Listen to others	1	2	3	4
Write effectively	1	2	3	4
Speak with impact	1	2	3	4
Demonstrate adaptability	1	2	3	4

Exhibit 3.3. Sample Needs Assessment Interview.

Instructions: Arrange a time to meet with each department manager. Prepare for each interview by developing open-ended questions to determine more completely what the manager believes should be happening, as well as to understand the current situation.

Here are some sample questions:

1. Describe the current situation as you see it. What have you observed that indicates there is a problem?

2. What specifically are the performers doing wrong? Doing right?

3. How often does the situation come up?

4. How many people need to change their performance?

5. What is the impact for their not meeting organizational objectives (cost, turnover, and so forth)?

6. Describe the desired performance.

7. What is the end result you are seeking from a training solution?

4

Create Goals and Objectives for the Program

ONCE YOU'VE DETERMINED the business need for training and gathered information about the learners and their situations, define exactly what the training is expected to change. To do this:

1. Record and substantiate the overall training program goal(s).

2. Write specific learning objectives.

Record and Substantiate the Overall Training Program Goal(s)

After the needs assessment work you've done, you'll know the overall goal the training intervention is intended to accomplish. A statement of a training goal should answer three questions:

- *Who* is the training intended for?

- *What* do they need to know?

- *How well* do they need to know it?

As with any goal, the more clearly you understand the end result you desire, the more likely you are to attain it. If you design a training program without knowing the answers to these three questions, you are much less likely to meet the specific training or business needs you've identified. For example, if you are developing training on new software, you would design a very different training solution for the senior management group than you would for the end-users. In the first case, your goal might be *to introduce the benefits and key features of our new software application to the senior management team.* The goal for the end-users might be *to instruct experienced software users on the steps they'll need to build the new company databases.*

By identifying two different goals, you'd end up with two *very* different training programs. Some other sample training goals are listed below:

- To instruct medical records analysts on the steps necessary for them to gather and document the data required by the American College of Surgeons.

- To provide an overview of the new benefits package to all company employees.

- To introduce new employees to the mission, key competitors, and corporate culture of the XYZ Company.

- To provide detailed instructions on the new diagnosis equipment for experienced field engineers.

The learning goal (or goals) define the overall purpose of the learning program. By recording the goals and sharing them with your internal customers, you will substantiate that the training solutions you plan to implement will indeed address their identified business needs. Exhibit 4.1 at the end of this chapter can be used to capture your learning goals and objectives.

Write Specific Learning Objectives

After you've determined your goal(s) for the training, the next critical step is to determine the specific learning objectives that will help you reach that goal. This step is very often overlooked, especially by inexperienced trainers or those who have never been exposed to the principles of instructional design. This step is as critical for designing training as it is for designing anything else, whether a new house, a software program, or the space shuttle. You wouldn't consider building a house without blueprints, a software application without end-user requirements, or the space shuttle without an engineering design. Yet many people develop training programs without any learning objectives. The result is a program that has little to no chance of actually meeting the learning or business need it was intended to address.

Learning objectives are different from goals—in terms of whom they're written for. A learning goal states *what the trainer intends to accomplish* (what business need will be addressed), while learning objectives indicate *what the participants will be able to do* after the training is complete. The more specific your learning objectives are, the more likely you'll design a program that will result in the behavioral changes you intend. Learning objectives complete the sentence: "At the end of the training session, participants will be able to. . . ." In general, learning objectives should be

- Measurable

- Attainable

- Precise

Measurable

Unfortunately, one of the most common verbs used when writing learning objectives is "understand." It is difficult to measure someone's *understanding* of a topic. You can, however, measure whether or not a participant can list, describe, recognize, or complete a series of sequential steps. If you use "understand" in a learning objective, you'll never know whether your training intervention successfully taught the participants what they had to know in order to meet the objective. For each learning objective you create, ask the question: "Could I test the participants' ability to accomplish this?"

Attainable

Expecting someone to be able to build a nuclear-powered rocket after two hours of classroom training is simply not realistic. When you write your learning objectives, keep in mind factors such as the time you have available for the training, the complexity of the content, and the experience of the participants.

Precise

Be very specific when writing your learning objectives. For example, be selective with the verb you choose. There is an enormous difference between being able to *recognize* a correct answer and being able to *recall* it, which is why multiple-choice tests are so much easier than fill-in-the-blank ones. If you want someone to be able to locate and follow a series of written procedural steps, you would create a very different program than if you wanted the same person to be able to follow the same steps in a stressful situation without any reference aids at all. To make writing your learning objectives easier, here is a list of behavioral verbs:

Adjust	Analyze	Apply
Choose	Compare	Conduct
Develop	Document	Explain
Identify	List	Locate
Match	Name	Organize
Predict	Prepare	Recall
Recognize	Select	Solve

One way to write and document learning objectives is to follow the steps below:

1. Jot down the topic areas your training has to cover in order to meet the stated goals.

2. List the behavioral steps your participants will have to follow within each topic area.

3. Look at each behavioral step individually and list the specific, detailed steps, if any, required to accomplish it, starting each with a verb.

4. List any specific knowledge a participant would require in order to accomplish each step and describe how he or she would have to demonstrate that knowledge (for example, recognize, list, describe in detail).

5. Combine the items in numbers 3 and 4 above and you now have a fairly complete list of learning objectives. Record these on a worksheet such as the one shown in Exhibit 4.1 at the end of the chapter.

6. Review the learning objectives you have so far with subject-matter experts to ensure they are accurate and complete and review them with management to obtain their buy-in.

Some sample goals with their learning objectives are listed below:

Learning goal: To instruct medical records analysts on the steps necessary for them to gather and document the data required by the American College of Surgeons.

Learning objectives: At the end of the session, the participants will be able to:

- Find all locations where medical records are kept within Trauma Services;

- Locate the information within the medical records to complete all required data fields; and

- Apply the specific diagnosis and procedural codes used by the department.

Learning goal: To provide an overview of the new benefits package to all company employees.

Learning objectives: At the end of the session, the participants will be able to:

- Name the three available health and dental insurance providers;

- Complete the insurance selection forms;

- Recognize the ten company holidays; and

- List the number of vacation and sick leave days they are entitled to use.

Learning goal: To introduce new employees to the mission, key competitors, and corporate culture of XYZ Company.

Learning objectives: At the end of the session, the participants will be able to:

- Recite and explain the company's mission statement;

- List and describe at least five of the company's six primary competitors; and

- Recognize at least three of the characteristics that make up the corporate culture and explain how each may impact the participants' ability to complete their job responsibilities.

Learning goal: To provide detailed instructions on the new diagnosis equipment to experienced field engineers.

Learning objectives: At the end of the session, the participants will be able to:

- Complete the initialization procedure;

- Follow the standard troubleshooting protocol;

- Successfully diagnose the eight most common equipment problems; and

- Complete the five finalization steps.

A learning objective should list the specific learner outcomes of the learning program. Use Exhibit 4.1 at the end of this chapter to complete this step in the process.

KEY POINTS

- Two critical components for a successful blended learning program are (1) clearly defined learning goals and (2) clear objectives.

- A goal defines what the program is intended to accomplish from the trainer's or organization's perspective.

- Learning objectives are written from the participants' perspective and complete the sentence, "At the end of this program, participants will be able to. . . ."

RESOURCES

Douds, A. F., & Ittner, P. L. (2003). *Train-the-trainer workshop: Instructor's guide* and *participant coursebook* (3rd ed.). Amherst, MA: HRD Press. A complete program for teaching non-trainers the skills they need to design and develop training, including a facilitator's guide, participant materials, hands-on activities, and case studies.

Lawson, K. (1998). *The trainer's handbook.* San Francisco, CA: Pfeiffer. Includes chapters on needs assessment, adult learners, training styles, writing learning objectives, and creating an instructional plan.

Rothwell, W. J., & Kazanas, H. C. (2003). *Mastering the instructional design process: A systematic approach* (3rd ed.). San Francisco, CA: Pfeiffer. A thorough step-by-step guide for the instructional design process; includes a CD-ROM with sample forms, checklists, activities, and PowerPoint® presentations.

Silberman, M., & Auerbach, C. (1998). *Active training: A handbook of techniques, designs, case examples, and tips.* San Francisco, CA: Pfeiffer. Includes information on how to assess learning needs, develop active learning objectives, and create active and effective exercises and presentations, as well as over two hundred real-life designs and case examples.

Exhibit 4.1. Learning Goal and Objectives Worksheet 1.

Instructions: Follow the steps below for every program you develop.

Step 1: Write a learning goal. Remember, your goal should answer these three questions:

- Who is the intended audience?
- What do they need to learn?
- How well do they need to know the content?

_____

_____

_____

Step 2: Draft the learning objectives, which need to be measurable, attainable, and precise.

At the end of the training, participants will be able to:

Objective: _____

_____

Possible learning solutions: _____

Objective: _____

_____

Possible learning solutions: _____

Objective: _____

_____

Possible learning solutions: _____

Exhibit 4.1. Learning Goal and Objectives Worksheet 1, *Continued*.

Objective: _____

_____

Possible learning solutions: _____

Objective: _____

_____

Possible learning solutions: _____

Objective: _____

_____

Possible learning solutions: _____

Objective: _____

_____

Possible learning solutions: _____

Objective: _____

_____

Possible learning solutions: _____

Step 3: (Complete this step at the end of the next chapter.) Identify which of your possible learning solution(s) might meet your learning objective and write it in the space provided after each objective.

5

Design the Blended Program

AFTER DETERMINING your goal(s) and specific learning objectives, you're now ready to outline a blended learning program that will meet your needs. This is done by determining which training solutions might work and then creating a training program design document that outlines the content to be covered and includes the training solution(s) that will be used.

Training Solution Options

With all of the options available, determining which training solution(s) to use may seem like a daunting task. To aid you in making a decision, in this chapter we provide three items: (1) basic definitions for nine of the most common training solutions; (2) a list and descriptions of factors to consider when selecting your training solutions; and (3) a matrix that includes both solutions and factors, with guidance as to which solutions may be most effective for your situation.

In this chapter, we provide descriptions of each of the training solutions that can be combined to form a blended learning program. Use this information to select the best solution(s) and to complete the design of your blended training program. Once your design is complete, you can turn to later chapters for more detailed information on how to develop and implement each of the specific training solutions.

Classroom Training

Classroom training refers to instruction that occurs in a physical classroom, with an instructor leading the delivery of course content to a group of participants. The instructor may be a training professional or a subject-matter expert (SME). This type of instruction is the most common form of training and is used most by organizations.

Subject-Matter Expert Training

Subject-matter expert training is the use of non-trainers with specialized knowledge in an area to develop and deliver training.

Assessment Instruments

An *assessment instrument* is a tool designed to solicit and communicate information about an individual, team, or organization. Assessment instruments can be in paper-and-pencil form or available via a computer.

Instructor-Led e-Learning

Any training where the primary delivery method is electronic and content is delivered via the Internet, intranet/extranet, audio or video technology, and/or CD-ROM is called e-learning. We make a distinction between two types of e-learning: instructor-led and self-study. *Instructor-led e-learning* (also known as synchronous e-learning) is where the primary delivery method is electronic, but with an instructor present to facilitate the training. The instructor-led e-learning solutions we discuss include online training, teleconferencing, videoconferencing, chat rooms, bulletin boards, and e-mail.

Self-Study e-Learning

We define *self-study e-learning* (also referred to as asynchronous e-learning) as those training solutions that are generally accessed by the learners without an instructor and in their own time. The specific methods we address in this book are technology-based training (TBT) programs (also known as computer-based training [CBT] programs) and knowledge databases.

Job Aids

Job aids are written resources for employees that contain information or processes to support work activity and guide or enhance performance. They are used to help employees perform specific tasks and often take the form of checklists, forms, reference manuals, or flowcharts. Job aids are often used for tasks that are performed infrequently or are new, so employees don't have to retain the information; they can simply look it up when they need it.

Mentoring

Mentoring is a partnership between two people where the individual with more experience (the mentor) shares skills, knowledge, and experience with an individual with less experience (the mentee or protégé). Mentoring provides employees with something no other learning opportunity does—a personal teacher and champion. Mentoring can be done in an informal manner, or it can be introduced through a formal program with multiple pairs of mentors and protégés working together.

Coaching

Coaching is an ongoing discussion between two people, in person, over the telephone, or via e-mail. Unlike coaching in sports, coaching used for corporate training purposes presumes that learners already possess the knowledge and skills they need, but for some reason are not applying them. The coach's job is to ask clients to examine reasons for their behavior and to guide them in identifying the internal obstacles, old beliefs, or patterns of thinking that can prevent them from changing their behavior.

On-the-Job Training

On-the-job training (OJT) is exactly what it sounds like—training conducted at the employee's job site, usually by a subject-matter expert who demonstrates the job or task to be learned. An on-the job training solution can be part of a larger, formal program or may simply involve one experienced worker showing a less experienced employee how to do part of his or her job.

Decision Factors—Definitions and Impact

Many factors influence the selection of the most effective training solutions. In this section, we briefly describe each of the factors and discuss how it may impact your decision.

Audience

Literacy of Learners. Consider the education level of your learners when deciding which solution to choose. Some off-the-shelf job aids, such as those that come with computer software programs, may be written at a higher education level than that of your employees. Recognize that even those who speak English proficiently may not be able to read at the same level and that many of today's companies have large populations of employees for whom English is a second language.

Resistant Learners. Resistant learners are employees who do not believe in or prefer not to use formal education. They do not see learning as positive or useful to their jobs or careers. They may have previously experienced frustration from inappropriate learning situations. Resistant learners may only resist classroom training or, as has been the case more recently, they may resist e-learning. Knowing your learner population and understanding which type of training solutions they may resist will help you select the most appropriate solution.

Computer Literacy of the Learners. Computer literacy refers to the employees' familiarity with computers. Knowing how to turn on a computer, insert a disc, and use a mouse to click and point are all components of computer literacy. Any e-learning solution requires that the learner have at least basic computer literacy. A more advanced familiarity with computers may be needed for more technical solutions.

Shift Workers. In today's environment, many organizations have shifts working around the clock and have adopted a variety of work schedules, including two or three shifts or ten-hour workdays with four-day workweeks.

If your organization has only a small number of employees working odd shifts, classroom training may not be the most effective for them; for example, holding a class for only three second-shift employees may not be efficient or practical. Conducting training using computers might be a better solution, as it would allow employees to take the class when it is more convenient for them.

Self-Directed Learners. Self-directed learners often don't require as much in-person support and contact, so e-learning solutions and job aids are often good solutions for them. Classroom training is highly desirable for those who are less self-directed, as the instructor can offer motivation, handle resistant learners, and provide structure.

Number of Trainees. In general, classroom training, knowledge databases, or e-learning solutions are best suited for a large number of trainees. For fewer learners, a one-on-one solution such as OJT, mentoring, or coaching is often more cost-effective.

Geographic Location of Learners. With employees often scattered around the globe and any of twenty-four time zones, organizations must consider training solutions that are flexible and that don't rely on physical proximity. Classroom training is most cost-effective if all or most of the participants are in the same location or if training can be delivered at multiple locations by a subject-matter expert. E-learning solutions are most commonly used for widely dispersed participants. Mentoring and coaching are also possibilities, although they may be limited to telephone contact, rather than in-person interactions.

Wide Diversity of Skill Level in Intended Audience. With a wide diversity of skill levels among your learners, one-on-one solutions such as mentoring or coaching are often the most effective because the training can be adjusted to meet the requirements of the individual learner. Other solutions such as classroom training or e-learning can be effective as well, if you design your training programs to be offered at different learning levels to meet the needs of basic, intermediate, and advanced learners.

Resources

Short Training Development Timeline. While each training solution requires thought and time to prepare, some solutions require more extended development time frames than others. For example, although off-the-shelf technology-based training (TBT) programs can be purchased quickly for common technical training needs, TBT programs intended to teach company-specific software require a great deal of development time. Many off-the-shelf classroom training programs are available that include facilitator guides as well as participant materials.

Availability of Subject-Matter Experts. When considering any of the solutions that require a subject-matter expert (SME), such as mentoring or SME-led classes, start by determining their availability. Being clear about expectations and time requirements will help you decide whether a solution that relies on SMEs is indeed going to be successful. For example, implementing a formal mentoring program and then discovering that insufficient number of mentors are available could spell disaster for the program.

Availability of Funds. Budget constraints often drive the choice of training solutions. The least expensive (and most commonly used) solution tends to be instructor-led presentations, with no participant interactivity. Sophisticated, custom-developed, technology-based training programs or knowledge databases tend to be the most expensive. Job shadowing and OJT can be inexpensive, since they often are implemented without much development time. However, as the number of participants increases, any of the solutions that are delivered one-on-one can be expensive when you consider cost of the participants' time.

Availability of Professional Trainers. Solutions such as classroom training require the availability of trainers to provide instruction. Therefore, access to trainers will impact your choice. Often SMEs are recruited to offer training instead of—or in tandem with—professional trainers.

Infrastructure

Computer Availability. Even with the increase in the popularity of e-learning, not all organizations have moved into the electronic age. If employees do not have access to desktop computers and you are considering an e-learning solution, you will have to provide laptop computers or a training room with computers.

Classroom Availability. Not all organizations are large enough to have dedicated space available for classroom training. Conference or meeting rooms can often be used, or hotels or public buildings such as libraries may have space available for rent. For frequent training sessions, it is important to have ready access to a classroom.

Content

Stable Course Content. The stability of the course content is an important factor too. If your content is stable, any solution requiring more development time, such as classroom training or technology-based training, may be a better choice.

Unstable Course Content. If the content is still in development or changes frequently by its nature, consider solutions that are relatively easy and inexpensive to update, such as online job aids, videoconferencing, teleconferencing, e-mail, or online training.

Volume of Material to Be Covered. Reflect on the amount of material to be taught as you make a decision about the optimal learning solution. If you are simply updating employees on a policy change, a four-hour class would be overkill, but a job aid may be sufficient. If you have six different topics to cover under the heading of management training, instead of a three-day class, consider a variety of solutions to add interest and to make the learning more effective.

Soft Skill Training Content. Soft skills, such as management or communication skills, are most effectively taught in person, so classroom training, coaching, or mentoring are excellent choices. Subject-matter expert training and OJT tend to be slightly less effective, because the person delivering the instruction may lack the training skills necessary to successfully model the desired behavior and provide constructive feedback.

Technical Training Content. E-learning solutions are most often used with technical training content and are generally quite effective, depending on the audience. Highly technical learners will demand a sophisticated look and feel to any e-learning solution; those new to using computers will want the individual support and instruction offered through solutions such as classroom training or OJT.

Decision Matrix

The decision matrix in Exhibit 5.1 at the end of the chapter has been designed to help you select the most effective solution(s) for your own blended training program. Instructions are included for using the matrix.

Once you've selected the solutions that suit your specific situation, use Exhibit 5.2, which is an updated version of Exhibit 4.1 that you partially completed at the end of Chapter 4. Record which training solution(s) would be appropriate to fulfill each specific learning objective, and list all that apply; you'll narrow the list of possibilities when you create your training program design document.

Training Program Design Documents

Start the process of creating a design document by looking at your learning objectives and the list of possible training solutions you just identified on the

Learning Goal and Objectives Worksheet in Exhibit 5.2. We've found it easiest to design a training program by creating a matrix that includes the topics, key points for each topic, expected duration (if applicable), and training
method(s). (Exhibit 5.3 at the end of the chapter has been provided for you
to use for this purpose.) To narrow the list of possible training solutions, consider which ones will best fit your organizational needs and be sure to include
a variety of training solutions. You may want to refer back to the factors on
your decision matrix to identify which are important for your organization's
needs. List which solution you select for each topic on the design document.

People prefer to learn in a variety of ways, and unless you make a specific
effort to offer a variety of methods, you'll tend to use only the one you prefer,
subconsciously assuming that everyone else prefers it too. Creating a design
document before you develop any of the solutions or materials ensures that
you offer a variety of methods without having to go back and rework a topic
later. If you are fairly new to blended learning, you might start out with classroom methods such as presentation, demonstration, reading, and discussion
and supplement them with one other training solution such as job aids or
e-mailed pre-work. More experienced trainers might want to add methods
such as games, puzzles, activities, and real-life simulations to the classroom and
a few training solutions in addition, such as job aids, technology-based training, and mentoring programs.

Additionally, your training will be far more effective if you design and
develop your program with adult learning principles in mind. In general,
adults:

- Learn more quickly when they can attach the new information to
  existing knowledge. The best way to address this is to provide "real-
  life" examples and to emphasize how the learning can be applied to
  the current situation.

- Will learn what *they* want to, not what *you* want them to. This tendency is entirely natural, and you can take advantage of it by relating the training to *learners'* goals. The more you can show how the

training will meet their goals, the more likely they will remember the information.

- Will learn more quickly when they can interact with the information. Encourage learners to share how they'll use the information by providing activities that help them to actively interact with the content and by providing real-life examples and scenarios whenever possible. Many inexperienced trainers will only lecture to their learners. Even with fancy software and graphics, the average adult can only listen passively for about ten minutes without falling mentally asleep; anything over ten minutes and their rate of retention becomes very low.

- Want to be respected. To make the training more effective, always treat the learners as partners in the learning process. Allow them to challenge and debate the ideas; respect their opinions; provide a safe environment in which they can fail when trying new skills; and encourage them to answer each other's questions, even when you know the answers.

It is essential to take the time to design the training program to meet whatever learning need you've identified. Many people skimp on their design and find that, while they may actually deliver a training program, it often doesn't result in any actual behavioral change.

KEY POINTS

- Training can be delivered using a variety of solutions, including classroom sessions, subject-matter experts, assessment instruments, self-study e-learning, instructor-led e-learning, job aids, mentoring, coaching, and on-the-job training.

- Selecting the most effective training solutions requires you to look at a variety of factors, such as the development time available, literacy of the intended participants, budget, location of the learners, and number of trainees.

- Creating a training program design document allows you to outline all of the content and possible solutions *before* actually developing the training. This ensures that you use a variety of training solutions (to meet the needs of various learning styles) and that you manage the process of developing the discrete components of your training program (covered in the next chapter).

Exhibit 5.1. Decision Matrix.

Instructions: To use this matrix, follow the steps below:

1. Review the definitions of the factors listed in the left-hand column (presented in this chapter, pages 46–50).

2. With a highlighter, mark those factors that are applicable to your current subject matter and participants.

3. Look across the row for each highlighted factor, and note which solutions have an X in the box.

4. Select one or more solutions from those that are marked. More than one X in the row indicates several excellent possible solutions for your training need.

Audience	Classroom	Assessment Instruments	Job Aids	Mentor	Coaching	OJT	Self-Study e-Learning	Instructor-Led e-Learning
Resistant learners	X			X	X			
Learners are computer literate		X	X				X	X
Learners not all on the same shift			X	X	X	X	X	X
Self-directed learners		X	X				X	X
Large number of trainees (26 or more)	X		X				X	X
Small number of trainees (25 or fewer)				X	X	X		
Location of learners—nearby	X			X	X	X		
Location of learners—scattered			X			X	X	X
Wide diversity of skill level in intended audience		X		X	X			

Resources								
Training development timeline is short			X			X	X	
SME availability	X			X	X	X	X	
Big budget (allows for external resource purchases)	X			X	X	X	X	X
Little budget	X			X	X	X	X	
Professional trainers available	X							X
Professional trainers unavailable			X	X			X	
Infrastructure								
Computer access/training room available	X			X	X	X	X	X
Classroom not available				X	X	X	X	X
Content								
Stable course content	X						X	X
Unstable course content			X					X
Minimal content to be delivered			X		X			X
Soft skill training content	X		X	X	X		X	
Technical training content			X			X	X	X

The Other Blended Learning. Copyright © 2005 by John Wiley & Sons, Inc. Reproduced by permission of Pfeiffer, an Imprint of Wiley. www.pfeiffer.com

Exhibit 5.2. Learning Goal and Objectives Worksheet 2.

Instructions: This is the same worksheet you began in Chapter 4. You've already written your goal and specific objectives; now go back to each objective and list which learning solution(s) would be appropriate to meet the specific learning need. You'll use these possibilities when you create your training design document.

Step 1: Write a learning goal. Remember, your goal should answer these three questions:

- Who is the intended audience?
- What do they need to learn?
- How well do they need to know the content?

_____

_____

_____

Step 2: Draft the learning objectives, which need to be measurable, attainable, and precise.

At the end of the training, participants will be able to:

Objective: _____

_____

Possible learning solutions: _____

Objective: _____

_____

Possible learning solutions: _____

Objective: _____

_____

Possible learning solutions: _____

Exhibit 5.2. Learning Goal and Objectives Worksheet 2, *Continued*.

Objective: _____

_____

Possible learning solutions: _____

Objective: _____

_____

Possible learning solutions: _____

Objective: _____

_____

Possible learning solutions: _____

Objective: _____

_____

Possible learning solutions: _____

Objective: _____

_____

Possible learning solutions: _____

Step 3: Identify which of your possible learning solution(s) might meet your learning objective and write it in the space provided after each objective.

Exhibit 5.3. Training Program Design Form.

Topic and Duration	Key Points	Method/Training Solution

6

Create and Coordinate the Individual Training Solutions

AFTER YOU HAVE SELECTED the individual solutions and outlined your blended learning program by creating a design document, the actual development work can proceed. The following are essential to the successful completion of the development process:

1. Coordinate the look and feel of the individual training solutions.

2. Manage the development process.

Coordinate the Look and Feel of the Individual Training Solutions

As the individual training solutions are being created, ensure that the components have a similar look or feel to them. Job aids, class materials, e-learning elements, and other components do not need to look identical, but they should be formatted in a comparable way. Using consistent graphic elements will create a familiar feeling across learning activities. If one training solution has already been developed and you create additional solutions to enhance it, you can either format the additional solutions to look like the original one or you can create a new look for all of the solutions and adjust or enhance the appearance of the original solution.

Something as simple as the consistent use of fonts, colors, and layouts may help the learners increase retention and more effectively move them from learning to actual behavioral change. In addition, if examples or scenarios are used in one component of the blended program, use the same or similar scenarios across all of the learning methods. This helps participants to connect what was learned in one training situation with what is being reinforced in the next.

The coordination is easier to do if one person is designing all of the materials. If you have multiple instructional designers, they should work together from a common set of design criteria to ensure they are using the same terminology and to make sure that the various solutions look similar.

Besides creating a similar look and feel, planning for the transitions from one training solution to another will enhance a blended program's effectiveness. Consider how each solution will be introduced and, when possible, use one solution to launch the next. For example, introducing a mentoring program through a classroom setting will help participants connect the two learning activities. Attaching job aids to an electronic notice about computer training may encourage participants to experiment with them prior to the e-learning session. This type of coordination will move your program from a series of discrete learning solutions to a truly blended program.

Manage the Development Process

At times a single person or team will complete the development process, and it will be relatively simple to manage the project. However, with robust programs encompassing a variety of solutions, multiple designers may develop different pieces of the blended program; in this case the role of project manager becomes critical. A project manager does the following:

- Creates and maintains a project plan, including specific tasks, timelines, and resources;

- Assigns the development work of each component of the program to a developer;

- Ensures each developer progresses according to the project plan; and

- Ensures all development is completed on time and within the budget.

These responsibilities are explained below.

Creates and Maintains a Project Plan, Including Specific Tasks, Timelines, and Resources. Project managers are responsible for the overall coordination of the development work and may or may not actually develop materials themselves. This role is separate from development work and is new to many instructional designers.

The easiest way to coordinate the development work is to create and maintain a project plan. If you're the project manager, use the design document as your guide and transfer the development tasks of the individual training solutions to a project plan. The project plan should include standard components, such as a list of the tasks to be completed. For each task, an expected start and end date, who is responsible, and how you'll know when it's completed (a measurement or deliverable) should be included. A sample project plan is shown in Exhibit 6.1. A blank project plan worksheet (Exhibit 6.2) is at the end of the chapter.

Assigns the Development Work of Each Component of the Program to a Developer. Depending on the organizational structure and the job responsibilities of the people involved, as a project manager, you may or may not have the authority to assign work; your responsibility may be limited to ensuring that the people who were assigned the tasks complete them. It's essential that the responsibility of the project manager be clearly defined. It's also essential that—no matter who assigns the work—the project manager must be given the authority to hold the team members accountable for completing the assigned tasks, with a process in place to report noncompliance to the person's manager if the person reports to someone else.

Ensures Each Developer Progresses According to the Project Plan. The easiest way to ensure that development progresses according to plan is to hold regular check-in meetings. We recommend that these be scheduled in advance, either weekly or bi-weekly, and that all team members participate. The agenda for these meetings can be simple and limited to an update of each person's scheduled tasks. Reviewing the progress this way ensures that any problems are caught early and that team members can be provided with whatever assistance they need to keep on track.

Another technique for keeping the development work progressing is to use standard, detailed checklists for each of the training solutions. Doing this provides a simple way for each developer to track his or her own progress and, if they keep copies of these development documents, provides a "paper trail." For example, the sample checklist in Exhibit 6.3 includes tasks that have to be completed (which can be the same as those on the project plan or be in more detail, if desired), the names of any supporting documentation, and a place to record the status of each task listed.

Ensures All Development Is Completed on Time and Within Budget. Since the success of a blended program depends on the interaction of its pieces, all development work must be completed according to the project plan. If job aids aren't completed in time to be introduced in the classroom session, for example, their usefulness could be dramatically lessened. Or if the basic content is to be covered in a computer-based training program and the program isn't completed on time, the classroom session intended to cover advanced content will have to be rescheduled.

Depending on your situation, the responsibility for the project's budget may be at different levels. You may be responsible for all aspects of the budget, including staff salaries, project materials, and vendor contracts. Or your budget responsibility may be indirect, limited to ensuring that all tasks are completed on time. In either case, keep in mind that one of the best ways to engage and maintain executive support is to link the development of training programs to business needs. Keeping management informed of the progress of development and state of the budget is an excellent way to keep them actively involved.

KEY POINTS

- Developing a successful blended program depends on two key concepts: coordinating the look and feel of the individual training solutions and managing the development process.

- Using the same look and feel throughout will enhance the program's effectiveness by increasing the likelihood that participants will transfer the learning to changes in behavior on the job.

- Managing the development process, especially for a large project, will ensure that any problems are caught and addressed early on.

RESOURCES

Kendrick, T. (2004). *The project management toolkit: 100 tips and techniques for getting the job done right.* New York: AMACOM. Includes processes based on the PMBOK (*Project Management Book of Knowledge*) on topics such as cost estimating and budgeting, communications and technology, individual and team goals, negotiation, management support, change and process improvement, quality assurance and control, risk management, and scheduling.

Martin, P., & Tate, K. (2001). *Getting started in project management.* Hoboken, NJ: John Wiley & Sons. Offers a practical approach to four phases of project management—initiation, planning, execution, and closure—and addresses basics such as the authors' seven keys to success, different approaches (directive or participatory), managing risk, and scheduling and budgeting techniques.

Portny, S. (2000). *Project management for dummies.* Hoboken, NJ: John Wiley & Sons. Basic introduction to project management covering the fundamentals, such as developing schedules, building a project team, working within the budget, managing risk, and motivating people who don't report to you.

Exhibit 6.1. Sample Project Plan.

Task	Start	End	Who	Deliverable
Classroom session				
Reserve training room and video equipment	7/15/05	7/16/05	Susan	Scheduled
Develop facilitator guide	8/30/05	10/15/05	Susan	Guide completed
Develop all participant materials, including training manual, discussion questions, icebreaker props	9/15/05	11/30/05	Susan	Materials completed
OJT				
Reserve training car	7/15/05	7/16/05	Jose	Reserved
Develop facilitator guide/instructor notes	8/30/05	10/15/05	Jose	Guide completed
Develop all participant materials, including job aids	9/15/05	11/30/05	Jose	Materials completed

Exhibit 6.2. Development Project Plan Worksheet.

Task	Start	End	Who	Deliverable

Exhibit 6.3. Sample Checklist.

Checklist for XYZ Training Development

Course Name: _____

Status: IP = in progress; xx/xx/xx = completed date; NA = not applicable

Status	Task and Steps	Document
	Analysis	
1-3-05	Review the Process Development Analysis.	
1-9-05	Conduct a task analysis to identify KSAs for the capability.	XYZ Process and Roles.xls
IP	Determine the audience.	XYZ Process and Roles.xls
	Conduct audience analysis to assess audience characteristics.	AudienceAnalysis.doc
	Review the documents to further identify course goals and objectives:	
	Templates	
	Samples (if any)	
	Methods (if any)	
	Tools (if applicable)	
	Document course goal and learning objectives.	Training Design.doc
	Conduct a review of the course goal and objectives; get management sign-off.	Training Review Form.doc
	Design	
	Determine the primary delivery method(s).	
	Determine the evaluation method(s).	
	Complete the high-level design.	Training Design.doc
	Conduct a review of the high-level design document and get management sign-off.	Training Design.doc

Exhibit 6.3. Sample Checklist, *Continued*.

Status	Task and Steps	Document
	Development	
	Review existing materials to leverage earlier work.	
	Develop classroom facilitator materials:	
	Facilitator guide	Facilitator Guide.doc
	PowerPoint presentation	Presentation.ppt
	Wall charts/other visuals	
	Level two evaluation (pre-tests/post-tests)	
	Develop classroom participant materials:	
	Manual	Manual.doc
	Handouts	Handouts.doc
	Job Aids	Job Aids.doc
	Locate level one evaluation form (smile sheet).	Evaluation 1.doc
	Conduct a review of the development deliverables.	

7

Implement the Blended Program

JUST AS THE DEVELOPMENT of the individual solutions has to be coordinated, the successful implementation of a blended learning program involves effectively *implementing* the individual training solutions as well as effectively *integrating* the discrete components. In this chapter we provide an overview of the fundamentals for implementing a blended learning program. See Chapters 9 through 17 for the implementation steps for each of the individual training solutions.

Your program launch could be relatively effortless if you have already been blending a couple of learning solutions, or it may be more complex if blended learning is new to your organization. If your organization is new to blended learning, carefully consider all of the following basic elements of an implementation plan:

- Clear business need
- Executive support

- Project manager
- Project team
- Project plan

Once blended learning becomes more established, these elements will tend to become part of your natural implementation.

Clear Business Need

While the determination of the business need is the first step in creating a blended learning program (see Chapter 3), maintaining a clear understanding of—and connection to—that business need is a key element in implementing your blended learning program. Establishing up-front how your program will result in solving a business problem or in achieving business goals is key to obtaining executive sponsorship.

Executive Support

Support from executives is necessary in order to obtain the resources needed to implement your program. If you plan to use solutions such as subject-matter experts, OJT, or coaching, you will likely be drawing from resources not usually used to provide training in the organization. In addition, as with any training program, you must have executive support to ensure that line managers will give employees time to participate in the blended learning program and to hold them accountable for the desired behavioral change. To engage and maintain executive support, you must (1) ask for their input; (2) link the training program to the business needs; and (3) keep them informed.

Ask for Their Input

People defend what they help create, so the best way to gain executive support is to actively solicit their input. Since managers are often the ones requesting training, ask them specific questions during the needs analysis phase about their expectations for the training and their perspectives on the training need and how it impacts the bottom line. Ask key executives to review training plans and/or materials and, if possible, have them formally approve any documents they review.

Link the Training Program to the Business Needs

The tools provided in Chapters 3 through 6 can help you link the business needs to your blended learning program. Since the program design is based on goals and objectives, which in turn are based on business needs, any blended program that is implemented using the steps from Chapters 3 through 6 will relate the needs to the program. In view of the fact that executives tend to focus on results, you can engage their support by demonstrating the results that your program is designed to achieve. The linkage can be demonstrated through an executive overview, in meetings, or through individual conversations.

Keep Them Informed

You can report on the progress of your blended learning programs through written or verbal updates. There are other ways to keep executives informed as well. For example, you can involve them by using them as guest instructors or by enlisting them to serve as mentors or coaches. Another approach is to consider sending out an executive summary of the results as the various blended solutions are completed and evaluated, along with any actions that are planned as a result. It's easier to sustain support if executives and managers are aware of the status of your program and of its success.

Project Manager

Blended learning programs that include several learning solutions require a project manager to make sure the discrete solutions are well coordinated and to serve as a focal point for questions and issues. The project manager is also responsible for the overall program evaluation. A more detailed description of the role of a project manager was included in Chapter 6.

Project Team

Unlike many individual training solutions, a blended learning program may require a project team to execute each element of the program and to make sure that the various training solutions are coordinated.

Project Plan

In addition to your project plan for the development of individual solutions, you'll want a project plan for the overall implementation that includes deadlines, milestones, and measures for implementing your blended learning program. The project plan should include which training solutions will be offered, to whom, and by when. This will drive the implementation of your blended program. A sample project implementation plan is shown in Exhibit 7.1 and a form, Exhibit 7.2, is provided for your use at the end of this chapter.

Depending on the size of your organization and the complexity of the blended learning program, you may also want a marketing component to promote blended learning as a solution to your business needs. Executive overviews explaining what blended learning is and why it's being implemented and employee e-mails promoting new methods for training could be part of such a marketing component. Review Chapter 6 for step-by-step instructions and additional samples.

KEY POINTS

- A more complex blended learning program requires a more complex implementation.
- A clear business need, executive support, and good project management are key to an effective implementation.

RESOURCES

Kendrick, T. (2004). *The project management toolkit: 100 tips and techniques for getting the job done right.* New York: AMACOM. Includes processes based on the

PMBOK (*Project Management Book of Knowledge*) on topics such as cost estimating and budgeting, communications and technology, individual and team goals, negotiation and management support, change and process improvement, quality assurance and control, risk management, and scheduling.

Martin, P., & Tate, K. (2001). *Getting started in project management.* Hoboken, NJ: John Wiley & Sons. Offers a practical approach to four phases of project management—initiation, planning, execution, and closure—and addresses basics such as the authors' seven keys to success, different approaches (directive or participatory), managing risk, and scheduling and budgeting techniques.

Portny, S. (2000). *Project management for dummies.* Hoboken, NJ: John Wiley & Sons. Basic introduction to project management covering the fundamentals, such as developing schedules, building a project team, working within the budget, managing risk, and motivating people who don't report to you.

Exhibit 7.1. Sample Project Implementation Plan.

Description	Start Date	End Date	Resources	Measures
Program designed	May 21	June 4	HR/IT	Design Document
Job aids drafted	June 14	June 30	IT	Completed
Class designed	June 20	July 7	HR	Design Document
Job aids piloted	July 1	July 10	Staff	Feedback
Mentors selected	July 5	July 12	HR	Fifteen confirmed
Job aids revised	July 11	July 21	IT	On website
Writing assignment created	July 10	July 12	HR	Complete?
Mentors trained	July 22	July 23	HR	Evaluations
Job aids sent to participants	July 24	July 24	HR	Complete?
Class announced	July 24	July 24	HR	Complete?
Class held and mentors assigned	August 1	August 2	HR	Evaluations
Assignments sent	August 2	October 2	HR/mentors	Complete?
Program evaluations	October 5	October 15	HR	Report

Exhibit 7.2. Project Implementation Plan Worksheet.

Description	Start Date	End Date	Resources	Measures

8

Measure the Results of the Program

A S WITH INDIVIDUAL TRAINING SOLUTIONS, we highly recommend that you measure the overall results once your blended learning program has been implemented. You can measure the results of the individual components of the blended learning solution or of the overall program. In either case, one of the most comprehensive and widely referenced models of training evaluation is Donald Kirkpatrick's *Evaluating Training Programs: The Four Levels* (1998). The four levels of this model are as follows:

1. *Reaction:* How much did the trainees *like* the program? This is generally accomplished with end-of-training evaluation forms (smile sheets).

2. *Learning:* What principles, facts, and concepts were *learned* during the training program? For example, having trainees demonstrate new skills is a fairly objective way to determine how much learning

has occurred. Where principles and facts are being taught, paper-and-pencil tests can be used.

3. *Transfer:* Did the trainees *transfer* the knowledge from class and change their behavior because of the training program? Observing employees complete a task they were unable to complete prior to training indicates a change in behavior.

4. *Results:* What were the *results* of the program in terms of factors such as reduced costs or reduction in turnover? For example, a learning program designed to reduce accidents on the job can be evaluated by measuring a percentage decrease in the number of accidents.

The most common is Level 1 because end-of-training questionnaires can provide quick answers and are easy and inexpensive to administer. However, responses to these evaluations do not necessarily measure the training's effectiveness. If you decide to use end-of-training surveys, you can make them more effective by having participants self-report on learning/application of learning. When creating a questionnaire, keep in mind that it should be short, easy to complete, and actionable (the feedback should provide you with information you can do something about). Level 1 instruments may be most useful for new training solutions or when using new instructors, as they may provide much-needed immediate feedback. See Exhibits 8.1 and 8.2 at the end of the chapter for sample Level 1 evaluation forms.

Level 2 evaluations will let you know whether your participants have learned the concepts that were presented in your training solution. Most sophisticated e-learning solutions include tests, and structured on-the-job training programs typically include a demonstration component that also measures learning. Other training solutions can incorporate written tests. See Exhibit 8.3 for a sample Level 2 evaluation form.

According to the 2004 ASTD State of the Industry Report, 74 percent of organizations use Level 1 evaluations, while only 31 percent use Level 2. Levels 3 and 4 tend to be more difficult to measure, with only 8 percent of companies reporting that they evaluate their training at Level 4.

When you choose to measure at Levels 3 and 4, the following suggestions could be useful:

1. *Conduct follow-up studies.* Study how training affects performance on the job. Focus on observable behavior whenever possible and include multiple sources of information. For example, if improved meeting effectiveness was an objective of your training solution, observe staff meetings to ensure they occur only when needed and to determine whether an agenda is followed (Level 3 evaluation).

2. *Set up control charts on key metrics.* Specify what you are trying to change, set up measurement systems, and track changes. For example, if you used existing quality data to conduct your needs assessment, you can measure a decrease in the error rate. If you are conducting customer service training, you may watch for a reduced number of customer complaints as evidence that training was effective. This type of data can be used for both Level 3 and Level 4 evaluation if you measure expenses and costs.

Exhibit 8.4 is an example of a Level 3 evaluation and Figure 8.1 shows Level 4 results. See Chapters 9 through 17 for specific information and examples of evaluation tools. However, just as with the implementation of training

Figure 8.1. Sample Level 4 Evaluation Results.

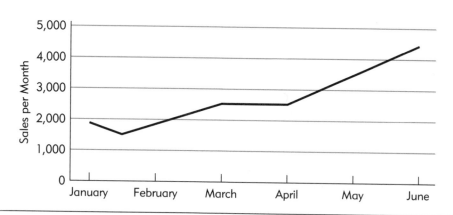

solutions, the evaluation of training solutions should be coordinated. If you are using a blended program with several learning solutions, it's possibly not a good use of resources to conduct a Level 1 evaluation on each discrete component. Participants may feel that they are being over-surveyed, and their responses might not prove to be an accurate reflection of their reactions to the training.

Since a well-constructed blended learning solution will have a direct tie to business results (step one), a Level 4 evaluation of the overall program is often the best way to appraise its effectiveness. For example, an increase in sales, a decrease in quality errors, or an improvement in cycle time are all examples of Level 4 results that can be measured.

KEY POINTS

- Measure the results of your blended learning program.

- Factors that can be measured range from satisfaction to return on investment.

- Tie your measures to business results.

RESOURCES

Kirkpatrick, D. L. (1998). *Evaluating training programs: The four levels.* San Francisco, CA: Berrett-Koehler. A primer for the basic issues involved in evaluating the effectiveness of training programs, containing numerous case studies from actual training programs.

Phillips, J. D. (2003). *Return on investment in training and performance improvement programs: Improving human performance* (2nd ed.). Burlington, MA: Butterworth-Heinemann. Guides you through a proven, results-based approach to calculating the return on investment in training and performance improvement programs.

Robinson, D. G., & Robinson, J. C. (1989). *Training for impact: How to link training to business needs and measure the results.* San Francisco, CA: Pfeiffer. Provides how-to strategies for implementing results-oriented training. Explains how to develop a collaborative, "client-consultant" relationship with line managers and to gain better management support for training efforts.

Exhibit 8.1. Sample Level 1 Evaluation Form 1.

Name of Class: _____

Name of Trainer: _____

Instructions: Fill out the following form to rate the course you just completed.

5 = Strongly agree; 4 = Agree; 3 = Disagree; 2 = Strongly disagree; 1 = NA

1. The course objectives were clear.   5   4   3   2   1

2. The instructor delivered the course material effectively.   5   4   3   2   1

3. After taking this course, I am now capable of   5   4   3   2   1
   [*course content,* for example, entering a job
   candidate into our tracking system]

   [*course content,* taken from objectives]   5   4   3   2   1

   [*course content,* taken from objectives]   5   4   3   2   1

4. I am confident I can apply what I learned in the   5   4   3   2   1
   course back on the job.

Most beneficial content in the course:

Suggestions for improvement:

Other comments:

Exhibit 8.2. Sample Level 1 Evaluation Form 2.

Participant Evaluation Form

Instructions: Please rate the following on a scale of 1 to 4 by circling your choices.

1 = Strongly disagree; 2 = Unsure; 3 = Agree; 4 = Strongly agree

Level of Learning   1   2   3   4

I am confident that [course content, for example, internal and external customer service] will improve as a result of my learning during this training.

Comments: _____

Job Performance   1   2   3   4

I am confident that I will be able to improve my on-the-job performance and incorporate the behaviors identified in this training.

Comments: _____

Job Satisfaction   1   2   3   4

I feel that my job is more meaningful and enjoyable due to the concepts and ideas that we discussed during the workshop.

Comments: _____

Participation   1   2   3   4

I felt free to talk and was encouraged to participate.

Comments: _____

Instructor   1   2   3   4

The instructor was well prepared, organized, interesting, a good listener, concise, responsive, controlled the group, and prevented distractions.

Comments: _____

Exhibit 8.2. Sample Level 1 Evaluation Form 2, *Continued*.

Training Materials (Handouts/Videos)   1   2   3   4

Varied, related to subject, appropriate amount, easy to understand.

Comments: _____

Program Content   1   2   3   4

Interesting activities, enough variety, realistic, organized, sensitive to needs of participants.

The most valuable part of this training:

_____

_____

_____

_____

The least valuable part of this training:

_____

_____

_____

_____

Other comments or suggestions:

_____

_____

_____

_____

Thank you very much!

Exhibit 8.3. Sample Level 2 Evaluation Form.

Driver Training

1. Before starting the ignition, what steps must you take?

2. When driving in rainy conditions, how far should you stay behind the car ahead of you?

3. What does a red flashing light at an intersection indicate?

4. When can you park at a green curb?

5. What is the legal speed limit on California's interstate highways?

6. What should you do if you are following a school bus that has its lights flashing?

Exhibit 8.4. Sample Level 3 Training Evaluation Results.

Call Center Training

	Before	After
Average time calls on hold	3.5 minutes	1 minute
Average number of call problems resolved without callback	12/week	4/week
Average number of resolutions on first call	30%	55%
Other criteria	xxx	xxx

PART 2

Individual Training Solutions

We tend to use learning solutions that are most familiar to us. However, as pointed out earlier in this book, those may not be the most effective solutions for our organization's learning needs. When conducting your needs assessment, the content to be delivered and the characteristics of the learners may suggest a learning solution with which you are less familiar.

This section provides details on nine of the more common individual training solutions. Each chapter provides you with a definition of the solution, its pros and cons, when to use the solution, how to implement it, and resource materials to aid you in using it. Since it is not within the scope of this book to provide every detail of implementing these solutions, we also list additional resources for those who want further information.

9

Classroom Training

Nigel had been working as a recruiter for a bank for seven years. He felt very comfortable recruiting on college campuses, representing the organization at job fairs, and calling his contacts to generate applicants for his bank's staffing needs. He was proficient at screening résumés, setting up interviews, and negotiating job offers.

Then his company decided to implement a new online recruiting system. The system required all recruiters to enter job requisitions into the computer, receive all résumés by electronic means, or scan them into the system, and it relied on recruiters to manage the applicant flow electronically.

While Nigel was computer savvy and used his e-mail and word processing software extensively in his work, he was not familiar with the new corporate software, nor was he comfortable keeping electronic files instead of paper copies of résumés. So he was the first in line to register for the training class that the HR department was offering to all recruiters.

The course was held at the downtown corporate headquarters and was attended by fifteen recruiters. In two half-days, they were taught how to log in to the new system, electronically enter a résumé, and track job candidates—all the way from receiving their applications through the actual hiring. The instructor explained the steps to follow, demonstrated how to use the system, and allowed participants to practice in the classroom. An incredible amount of information was covered, and the participants were sent home with a reference guide for their use back on the job.

Fortunately, the training was held immediately prior to the transition to the new online system. In addition, participants were asked to try a test version of the new program when they returned to their office. They were contacted by an "imaginary" job applicant and were required to enter the candidate into the system and to simulate the interviewing and hiring process. This allowed each recruiter to test his or her knowledge of the software before the system went "live."

When the system was implemented two days later, Nigel made extensive use of his classroom learning, the practice experience, and the reference guide to enter, track, and schedule candidates. While it was not as easy or comfortable for him as the old manual system, he was able to maneuver through the various computer screens and, within a week, was successfully entering and tracking job candidates. Other recruiters, who had opted not to attend the classroom training but to use the reference guide only, found themselves calling on Nigel and the others who had attended class to assist them with the new processes.

What Is Classroom Training?

Classroom training refers to instruction that occurs in a physical classroom, with an instructor delivering course content to a group of participants. It can include a variety of training methods such as group discussion, presentation, demonstration, games, and simulations.

In this chapter we focus on classroom training as the heart of blended learning. Classroom training is widely considered the most accepted form of training in organizations. Some pros and cons of the method are listed below.

Pros

- Is widely accepted;

- Provides for interaction with the instructor and other participants, allowing for clarification of points and quick response to questions;

- Allows the trainer to provide immediate feedback to the learners on their skill development;

- Can be affordable if course materials (for example, training videos) and in-house instructors are available;

- Provides high retention rates when materials are presented in an interactive format; and

- Can generate enthusiasm for the application of the subject matter being taught.

Cons

- Can require travel expenses if trainees are not all at one site;

- May require multiple sessions if a large number of participants exist, as typical corporate classrooms hold a maximum of twenty-five participants;

- Can be expensive per person when you have a small number of participants; and

- Requires a physical training room, which not all organizations have.

When to Use Classroom Training

Managers or employees will often ask for classroom training as a solution to a problem, but until the problem is understood in greater detail, offering this form of training can be a costly and fruitless endeavor. As we emphasized in Chapter 3 of this book, before implementing any training, you should conduct a needs assessment to decide whether a need for training exists, the nature of the content for the training program, and the appropriate training solution(s).

Classroom training is appropriate when you have a critical mass of people who all require the same skill, knowledge, or information and when a skilled trainer/facilitator is available to deliver the content. Classroom training is also appropriate when there is a desire for performance improvement or when there are new processes or tools to be introduced to employees. Additionally, soft skills or other skill development requiring practice and face-to-face feedback are excellent choices for classroom training.

When the employees who require the skill are in the same location, classroom training can be the most cost-effective method of transferring knowledge, as there is no travel time or expense. Classroom training may also be the appropriate solution when employees are geographically dispersed; but in these situations, you may want to consider blending it with distance-learning technologies (see Chapter 12, "Instructor-Led e-Learning").

Instructors or trainers can be found either inside or outside of the organization. Access to qualified individuals is an important element in determining whether classroom training is the appropriate method to address a learning need. Training departments in some organizations are segmented into instructional designers and deliverers; each of these roles has its own skill set. Both require the ability to apply adult learning theories, the instructional designers in the development of the solution(s) and the deliverers in the actual implementation of the training. In addition, instructional designers need proficiency in the design of training activities while deliverers require effective presentation and facilitation skills.

Ability to Apply Adult Learning Principles. Trainers should be well-versed in adult learning principles and be able to apply them to support the learning process. Instructional designers must also collect information from various sources to determine whether an actual training need exists and to use the information to design effective training solutions. We include additional information about adult learning principles in Chapter 10, "Subject-Matter Expert Training."

Proficiency in the Design of Training Activities. An effective instructional designer must understand and apply the core elements of training design—applying a variety of methods and approaches in the development of the class.

Effective Delivery Skills. Finally, a trainer has to be effective at delivering course content, managing course participants, giving clear instructions, facilitating discussions, and demonstrating new skills.

Note: In organizations where one trainer fulfills all roles from needs assessment to delivery, he or she will have to have all of the skills listed above.

How to Implement Classroom Training

In addition to determining needs, which is common to all training solutions, there are four basic steps to implementing classroom training:

1. Determine who will coordinate.
2. Determine who will conduct the training.
3. Develop and deliver the class(es).
4. Evaluate the training.

1. Determine Who Will Coordinate

The human resources (HR) department typically manages the training function, but if a specific department has a technical training need, it's not uncommon for that department to take responsibility for the coordination. In larger organizations, HR generally will handle the needs assessment, development, and delivery of classroom training. They may develop and deliver the training, use off-the-shelf training products, hire external trainers to conduct training, or use some combination of these options. The use of line managers or subject-matter experts (see Chapter 10, "Subject-Matter Expert Training") is also common.

Before undertaking a classroom training initiative, it is important to determine who will coordinate the efforts and to define his or her role in the process. You should determine which part of training the coordinator will provide and which parts will be parceled out to others within or outside of the organization. By way of example: Qualcomm, a digital and wireless technology company, has a training department that is primarily responsible for assessing training needs and then hiring external trainers to meet those needs. In contrast, Unisys, a worldwide information technology services and solutions company, has a staff of consultants who are responsible for everything from needs assessment through course delivery and evaluation.

2. Determine Who Will Conduct the Training

Larger organizations are more likely to have an internal training staff, while smaller organizations often have to rely on other sources. You must determine who is best suited to develop and deliver the training for your organization. The options include your in-house training staff, a line manager or subject-matter expert (SME), or an external trainer. The decision will not only be influenced by the size of your organization, but also by the subject matter, budget, and time available.

Using in-house trainers is the best solution if you have people who have the necessary training skills and if they have the time to develop and deliver the training within your time frame. If time is of the essence and you have no one with subject-matter expertise, it may be better to hire an external trainer who is also a subject-matter expert, who already has developed a class on the content, and who could fairly quickly customize it for your audience. If you do have internal subject-matter experts, you can also have them develop and deliver training, but this will take more time than the other options. The benefit is that SMEs are familiar with the organization and the employees who need to learn the subject. They have the best ability to customize the course material for the learners.

If subject-matter expertise is not available, another option is to purchase training materials, which are available for some of the more common training topics such as communications or customer service skills. Known as off-the-shelf training, these materials generally include an instructor's guide, participants' manuals, and overhead transparencies to use in conducting classroom training.

3. Develop and Deliver the Class(es)

Once the coordinator and trainer have been identified, the course content has to be developed. Since so many books have been written on instructional design, we will simply highlight the fact that the most effective classes incorporate a variety of delivery methods within the course. Therefore, the training will be most effective if you use a combination of methods such as lecture, examples, discussion, application, reading, observation, and practice. Sample classroom training templates are included at the end of this chapter in Exhibit 9.1. The use of visual aids such as flip charts or presentation software can also increase the effectiveness of the training and meet the needs of the more visual learners. (See Chapter 5, "Design the Blended Program," for more information.) If time allows, pilot new classes to ensure that the content flows well and to make certain that the participants who attend the pilot session learn the content.

In addition, you can increase the likelihood that the information will be applied on the job through post-classroom work such as on-the-job training. Exercises such as the one Nigel from our earlier example completed with the test software is one example of such follow-up work. You could also ask participants to report back to you when they have their first opportunity to apply the content in order to receive coaching on how to use what they learned. You could also contact managers and ask them to follow up with their employees to reinforce what was learned in the classroom. Finally, participants can be asked to share what they learned with their colleagues. This tends to make them more attentive in the classroom and encourages them to apply what they have learned so that they can act as role models for others afterward.

4. Evaluate the Training

As with all learning solutions, you'll want to conduct an evaluation once the classroom training is complete. As discussed in Chapter 8, "Measure the Results of the Program," Donald Kirkpatrick's (1989) model for training evaluation is one of the most inclusive and well-used models. Here is how you can apply his model to classroom training:

Level 1: Reaction   If measuring learner reaction is important to you, you will most likely use an end-of-course survey. While some trainers prefer to send out evaluations a few days following the class, your response rate will be higher if you distribute the evaluations while the learners are still in the classroom. Be sure to allow adequate time at the end of your class for respondents to complete the evaluation. Open-ended questions take more time to answer, but provide a quality of feedback that isn't possible by having learners simply indicate a rating.

Level 2: Learning

Evaluating at this level will show you what the participants actually learned in your class. You can measure learning through the use of tests or by having employees demonstrate a new skill. When using tests in the classroom, be aware that some learners have test anxiety. To address this, be sure to communicate at the start of the class that there will be an evaluation (stay away from using the word "test"). You may also want to let students work together when answering questions. If you plan to have students demonstrate a skill, schedule a practice session before asking them to officially demonstrate it. The goal is for every participant to answer all of the questions correctly or to demonstrate 100 percent proficiency when using a new skill.

Level 3: Transfer

To evaluate the transfer of knowledge, you measure whether the job behavior of the trainees changed as a result of a class. This cannot be measured in the classroom, but has to be measured back on the job. The instructor or the trainees' manager can conduct this level of evaluation.

Level 4: Results

The results of a class in terms of factors such as reduced costs or reduction in turnover can be measured following classroom training. It's important that you consider how you will measure results when you are developing your classroom goals and learning objectives. For example, a class designed to teach general customer service skills would not necessarily reduce the time that customers were kept on hold. If reducing hold time is the desired result, the course has to be designed to teach the specific customer service skills and techniques that will address that goal.

KEY POINTS

- Classroom training, occurring in a classroom with an instructor, is the most popular form of instruction in organizations.

- Determine who will coordinate and deliver training in your organization.

- Consider adult learning principles when designing classes.

- The four levels of evaluation can be applied to the classroom.

RESOURCES

Kirkpatrick, D. L. (1998). *Evaluating training programs: The four levels.* San Francisco, CA: Berrett-Koehler. A primer for the basic issues involved in evaluating the effectiveness of training programs, containing numerous case studies from actual training programs.

Mitchell, G. (1998). *Trainer's handbook: The AMA guide to effective training.* New York: AMACOM. A handbook on training from the basics of writing lesson plans to the challenges of training management.

Pike, B. (2003). *Creative training techniques.* Amherst, MA: HRD Press. An approach that uses adult learning principles to help people learn through instructor-led training.

Piskurich, G. M., Beckschi, P., & Hall, B. (2000). *ASTD handbook of training design and delivery.* New York: McGraw-Hill. A comprehensive guide to creating and delivering a variety of types of training programs.

Silberman, M. (1995). *101 ways to make training active.* San Francisco, CA: Pfeiffer. Strategies and techniques for classroom training, including individual and group exercises designed to enliven training and deepen retention.

Exhibit 9.1. Sample Classroom Training Templates.

Half-Day Course

20 min.	Introductions/review learning objectives
1 hour	Lecture/demonstration on content
1 hour	Discussion on application
10 min.	Break
1 hour	Practice/feedback
30 min.	Review

Full-Day Course

20 min.	Introductions/review learning objectives
1 hour	Lecture on content
1 hour	Demonstration or video of content
10 min.	Break
1 hr. 30 min.	Discussion and prepare for practice
1 hour	Lunch
1 hour	Practice
1 hour	Feedback on practice
30 min.	Application planning
30 min.	Review

10

Subject-Matter Expert Training

Julie was not happy. Her job kept her extremely busy, and now she was being asked to train the new employees. She just didn't have time to baby-sit a bunch of new workers, and where was she supposed to find the time to pull together training materials anyway? The HR representative and her boss told her they chose her to be the subject-matter expert trainer be-cause she was so approachable and because people respected her. That was great and she did appreciate it, but did they give her any extra time to get the stuff done? Or was she expected to just fit it in on top of her other responsibilities? Scott—the HR person—said he'd help, but how much help would he be, since he didn't know any of the material she had to teach?

Rather grudgingly, Julie attended the train-the-trainer session Scott had arranged. He started out the meeting by thanking them all for agree-ing to help and by repeating that they had been chosen because they were well liked and approachable and because people tended to seek them out for help anyway. He didn't say much about their expertise, other than to say that sometimes the best teachers were people who did NOT know the most about the topic. In fact, sometimes those people were the worst teachers because they either talked way over the new employees' level or because they were so hung up on being the experts that they didn't want to share their knowledge. Julie grinned at this; she'd worked with a couple of people just like that.

One of the things that Scott taught them was how to come up with learning objectives—to start with listing what behaviors the new employees had to learn, then to narrow the focus of the training to include the least amount of information they would need. As he put it, "Answer any question they ask, but offer only what they need to know." He pointed out that adults can only learn a certain amount of information at a time, so if you tell them everything you know, you'll only frustrate and confuse them. After thinking about it, Julie thought she could see the sense in that.

Scott also gave them a blueprint for their training in a variety of forms; depending on how each person worked, he or she could choose paper forms, a presentation software file, or a word processing document. He then gave them time to complete their blueprints in the class and scheduled a follow-up meeting for those who wanted to work a bit more and receive feedback later. He also instructed them on effective presentation skills and allowed them the opportunity to practice their skills. At the end of the class, Julie was pleasantly surprised; she had a complete outline of what she wanted to say, a few handouts she knew would be helpful after her class was over, and even an evaluation form. While she still had to negotiate with her boss for someone to cover some of her other responsibilities, she now felt much better prepared to be an effective instructor and take on the new employee training.

What Is Subject-Matter Expert Training?

While subject-matter expert (SME) training is actually a form of classroom training, we include it as a separate solution due to the special issues that come up when using SMEs to design and deliver training. Training expertise can be broken into two primary skill areas: One is the ability to effectively facilitate a learning environment; the other is having specialized knowledge in the area you're trying to teach. SME training is the use of non-trainers with specialized knowledge in an area to develop and deliver training.

Organizations usually select trainers based either on their training skills or on their expertise in the subject matter. Organizations that hire professional trainers to deliver training capitalize on those people's training skills and assume that they will learn the content. Organizations may also ask their subject-matter experts to deliver training and either assume they have training skills or—all too often—don't recognize the need for any specialized skills at all. Both training skills and subject-matter skills are equally important, and the most effective training will be delivered by a trainer who has both. The pros and cons of subject-matter expert training are listed below.

Pros

- SME trainers have expertise in the content and (usually) have instant credibility with the learners;

- SME trainers can provide real-life scenarios and are able to apply the content directly to the workplace; and

- Participants often know the SME trainers, so rapport is already established.

Cons

- SME trainers may lack effective presentation and facilitation skills;

- SME trainers may bring the stress of their job responsibilities to the learning environment; and

- Participants often know the SME trainers, which could be a problem if the SMEs are not well respected.

When to Use Subject-Matter Expert Training

Using subject-matter experts to deliver training is most useful when:

- The content of the training is highly technical;

- The content changes frequently;

- The content is very organization-specific;

- No budget exists for hiring outside trainers;
- Training is only needed infrequently; and/or
- Training is needed on short notice.

How to Implement Subject-Matter Expert Training

The steps to effectively use SMEs to deliver training are outlined below.

Phase I: Preparation

1. Determine the need and purpose for SME training.

2. Select subject-matter experts.

3. Obtain management support for the program.

4. Teach basic adult learning principles to the SMEs.

Phase II: Implementation

5. Help the SMEs determine the specific learning objectives.

6. Offer templates for agendas, facilitator guides, job aids, and/or handouts.

7. Provide scheduling and logistics assistance.

Phase III: Evaluation

8. Compile, summarize, and report the results.

Phase I: Preparation

1. **Determine the Need and Purpose for SME Training.** Review the When to Use section above to decide whether SME training is the appropriate solution. Don't assume that SME training is the best or only answer. Alternative solutions include creating job aids, designing a mentoring program, and/or using professional trainers. Remember, too, if the need is due to factors other than new skill development, providing training can result in a waste of resources, employee frustration, or even making a bad problem worse. (For more details on how to determine the best solution, see Chapter 5, Design the Blended Program.)

2. **Select Subject-Matter Experts.** Selecting SMEs with the appropriate skills is probably the most critical decision you'll make in determining the success of

a SME training program. All too often the task is delegated to someone who has the time available or who is considered to be a content expert, without any consideration being given to training skills. To ensure that the training is effective, make sure your SMEs either already possess effective training and facilitation skills or are willing to develop them. Be cautious that your SMEs don't assume that their role is to conduct training in a hierarchical (trainer up, participant down) manner, rather than as a shared learning experience. If they do the former, they often unintentionally and subconsciously treat participants in ways that discourage learning, such as by becoming defensive when the learners challenge the information, by treating them in a demeaning manner, or by discouraging them from asking questions. Challenging information and asking questions are perfectly natural behaviors on the part of adult learners; if the SME doesn't allow these behaviors or acts in an otherwise hierarchical manner, the effectiveness of the training will be compromised.

Keeping all this in mind, watch for these attributes when selecting your SMEs:

- Ability to treat others with respect;
- Willingness to be challenged in a learning environment;
- Willingness to encourage questions and discussion;
- Being known as an "answer person"—someone to whom people naturally gravitate when needing information;
- Willingness to share information;
- Adequate content expertise;
- Time availability to prepare and conduct the training session; and
- Support for the program from his or her manager.

3. Obtain Management Support for the Program. Asking a SME to provide training will require a time commitment outside of the employee's regular job, sometimes a substantial amount, depending on the depth and amount of content to be covered. Because of this, it's important to ensure management support of the program before beginning implementation, especially from the employee's immediate manager or supervisor.

4. Teach Basic Adult Learning Principles to the SMEs. If you've selected SMEs using the criteria above, they won't need too much training on adult learning principles; they'll be using many of them already, even if they couldn't name or describe them. However, we recommend that you offer the information anyway; experience has shown that these principles can be taught multiple times to the same person, with each session resulting in deeper understanding and a greater ability for delivering effective training.

Adult learning principles are summarized below. In general, adults:

- Learn more quickly when they can attach the new information to existing knowledge. The best way to address this is to provide "real-life" examples and to emphasize how the learning can be applied to their current situation.

- Will learn what *they* want to, not what *you* want them to. This is entirely natural and you can take advantage of this tendency by relating the training to *learners'* goals. The more you can show how the training will meet their goals, the more likely they will remember the information.

- Will learn more quickly when they can interact with the information. Encourage learners to share how they will use the information, by providing exercises that persuade them to interact actively with the content and by providing real-life examples and scenarios whenever possible. Many inexperienced trainers will only lecture to their learners. Even with fancy software and graphics, the average adult can only listen passively for about ten minutes without falling mentally asleep; anything over ten minutes and their rate of learning retention becomes very low.

- Want to be respected. To make the training more effective, always treat the learners as a partner in the learning process. Allow them to challenge and debate the ideas, respect their opinions, provide a safe environment in which they can fail when trying new skills, and encourage them to answer each other's questions, even when you know the answers as well.

A simple exercise to teach these principles includes just five steps and can be used with a group of learners or a single individual:

1. Ask SMEs to remember the worst teacher/trainer they ever had and to make a few notes describing this person. This could be an elementary school teacher, college professor, or training facilitator. Have them picture the setting, the trainer, themselves, what they did in the class. Give them three minutes or so, then ask who would be willing to share his or her worst experience.

2. Record the answers on a flip chart, whiteboard, or piece of paper, looking for answers such as "feeling talked down to," right/wrong answers, or lecturing as the only training method.

3. Then ask the SMEs to think about the best teacher/trainer they'd ever had and have them record a few notes. Give them another three minutes or so; then ask for a volunteer to share.

4. Again record the answers, looking for items such as a relaxed atmosphere, actively working with the content, and real-life examples.

5. Summarize the adult learning principles listed above, tying them back to the answers provided by the SMEs. Point out that their learners will be no different and will want to be treated with the positive qualities they've identified.

Phase II: Implementation

5. Help the SMEs Determine the Specific Learning Objectives. Most SMEs won't have any idea how to create learning objectives. You can help them by briefly explaining the purpose and benefits of using learning objectives (refer to Chapter 4, Create Goals and Objectives for the Program, for more information) and by assisting them in writing the learning objectives themselves. You can do this through:

- *Observation*—For job skills, shadow someone who is performing the job and list the tasks, knowledge, and/or skills he or she exhibits.

- *Focus groups*—Invite all those with expertise in the content area and allow them to brainstorm the list of objectives. Keep in mind that, as experts, they may tend to list objectives for everything they know and not limit themselves. You can help them focus on just those objectives needed by people learning at a more basic level.

- *One-on-one discussion*—Arrange a meeting with each SME and question him or her about the knowledge, skills, and abilities needed.

6. **Offer Templates for Agendas, Facilitator Guides, Job Aids, and/or Handouts.** Previously prepared templates can greatly reduce preparation time and increase a SME's feelings of confidence. They can also result in materials that are more professional looking, consistent in format, and user-friendly. Samples are included in Exhibits 10.1–10.3 at the end of this chapter.

7. **Provide Scheduling and Logistics Assistance.** SMEs usually take on a training role in addition to their regular job responsibilities. You can aid them greatly by scheduling training rooms and equipment, finding the best times available to the learners, and registering participants for sessions. Set up the training room with course materials, name tags, and evaluation forms. This will save time as well as reduce the stress associated with delivering training for the first time.

Phase III: Evaluation

8. **Compile, Summarize, and Report the Results.** As with any training method, it's important to measure success. The most common way of evaluating the success of a training program is by asking the participants to complete an evaluation form at the end of each session. Remind the SMEs to allow time for the participants to do so (the rate of return when participants take the evaluations away to complete is very low). We recommend that you provide a form for SMEs to use and decide whether you wish the evaluations to be returned to the SME or to a central location. A Level 1 sample evaluation is provided in Exhibit 10.4; additional sample evaluations are included at the end of Chapter 8. When evaluating training conducted by subject-matter experts, we recommend that you gather feedback on their delivery skills. Sharing this feedback in person provides you with an opportunity to coach them to improve their training skills.

See Chapter 8, "Measure the Results of the Program," for additional information about measuring training success.

KEY POINTS

- Successful trainers must have expertise in two separate areas—the ability to effectively facilitate a learning environment and specialized content knowledge.

- If needed, offer your SMEs education in train-the-trainer topics such as presentation and facilitation skills and adult learning principles.

- To increase the quality of your SME training, make sure your SMEs have the availability, manager support, and interest to develop and deliver training.

- SMEs can offer real-life scenarios, instant credibility, and on-the-job support.

RESOURCES

Douds, A. F., & Ittner, P. L. (2003). *Train-the-trainer workshop: Instructor's guide* and *participant coursebook* (3rd ed.). Amherst, MA: HRD Press. A complete program for teaching non-trainers the skills they need to design and develop training, including a facilitator's guide, participant materials, hands-on activities, and case studies.

Elengold, L. J. (2001). *Info-line 250106: Teach SMEs to design training.* Alexandria, VA: ASTD. A step-by-step approach that teaches SMEs about adult learning theories and how to design an effective training program.

Goad, T. W. (1997). *The first-time trainer: A step-by-step quick guide for managers, supervisors, and new training professionals.* New York: AMACOM. A guide for people new to training, with essential theory, tools, tips, and real-world examples.

Weiss, E. (1996). *The accidental trainer: You know computers, so they want you to teach everyone else.* San Francisco, CA: Pfeiffer. A guide designed for computer experts who are asked to design and deliver training; contains checklists, questionnaires, and other hands-on tools.

Exhibit 10.1. Sample Facilitator Guide.

Introduction	*Introductions*
15 minutes	• Introduce yourself (briefly).
8:30 to 8:45	• Direct them to the agenda on page 1 in their manuals.
	• Explain that this session is designed as two four-hour sessions and talk about what you'll cover in each session.
	• Explain (briefly) about breaks, other housekeeping issues.
	• Explain how time is to be tracked in TRS/Project Central.
	Icebreaker
	• Ask the participants about their expectations for the session and record them on a flip chart. Emphasize that this session focuses on the Requirement Management process: there will be a separate session on the tool.
Requirements Management Benefits	Talk briefly about the major reasons for developing a standardized process on Requirement Management:
20 minutes	• The crucial nature of Requirement Management in preventing failure and defects downstream.
8:45 to 9:05	• That this process is the standard—the minimum—but it has flexibility built in. You can do more than this if your project or customer requires it.
The Core Four	Talk briefly about Karl Wiegers's Model—The Core Four (a hierarchy of Requirements)
10 minutes	
9:05 to 9:15	• The Why: Business Requirements
	• The What: User Requirements
	• The Detailed What: Functional Requirements
	• The How: Technical Requirements
	Remind the group that "requirements" are more than just functional requirements.
	Answer any questions before going on.

Exhibit 10.1. Sample Facilitator Guide, *Continued*.

Initiation **Output Documents** 30 minutes 9:15 to 10:45	Explain that you'll cover the three documents drafted during the IN process: • Statement of Work • Project Plan • High-Level Requirements Document Remind them that the SOW and the Project Plan are preconditions for the project's approval and funding, but the allocated requirements of the HLRD are the basis for their work in gathering and managing requirements. Direct them to the information on page 3 as you present information about the three documents. FAQ: Who is responsible for creating the HLRD? Answer: System Analysts (with input from the business)
	Ask them: Are you currently using documents like these? Expect answers such as: • We gather this information, but in a different format. • We talk to users without using formal documents. • Analysts don't have templates; they figure it out on their own. Emphasize the importance of a standard and repeatable way to start the requirement management effort.

Exhibit 10.2. Sample Training Agenda.

Agenda

Welcome and Introductions

Theme: Discovering Our Strengths, Celebrating Our Successes

Portrait of the Last Year—timeline exercise

Portrait of the Last Year—mosaic

Lunch

A Look at Ourselves—energy and communication exercise

A Look at Ourselves—MBTI

Future Applications and Lessons Learned

Exhibit 10.3. Sample Handout.

Media and Materials: Handouts

Handouts are written materials prepared in advance and distributed to the learners during the training. The information covered in a handout can be used during the training and/or retained for use afterward.

Handouts are important training aids to consider, particularly if you want to:

1. Have learners use the information at a later time (during the training or after the training).
2. Allow learners to absorb information at their own pace.
3. Eliminate the need for learners to memorize or take notes.

The first step in developing a handout is to decide on the format you will use for presenting the information. One of the choices you have is to present the information in paragraph form. (The information you are reading right now is an example of information in paragraph form.) It has its place in handouts, but it also has drawbacks.

A major drawback of information in paragraph form is that it is visually less appealing to the reader than other formats. This is particularly true if you are presenting a lot of information. Other formats can be used that are more interesting to readers and do a better job in communicating your information under certain conditions.

Three handout formats that are particularly helpful as training aids are

1. Decision charts
2. Checklists
3. Worksheets

Exhibit 10.4. Sample Evaluation Form for SME Training.

Instructor: _____   Course: _____   Date: _____

Assistant: _____   Location: _____

Instructions: Please rank each of the following as

   1 = Very poor, 2 = Poor, 3 = Not sure, 4 = Good, 5 = Very good

If you wish, you may add comments in the space to the right. Thank you!

Area	Rating	Comments
Preparation		
Organization	1 2 3 4 5	
Design, effectiveness, use of materials	1 2 3 4 5	
Knowledge of program and materials	1 2 3 4 5	
Presentation Abilities		
Rapport	1 2 3 4 5	
Energy level/enthusiasm	1 2 3 4 5	
Voice: speech, articulation, habits	1 2 3 4 5	
Body dynamics/language	1 2 3 4 5	
Effective use of whiteboards and/or projected materials	1 2 3 4 5	
Level of professionalism	1 2 3 4 5	
Honesty/genuineness	1 2 3 4 5	
Training Skills		
Pacing	1 2 3 4 5	
Communication skills: clear, thorough, accurate	1 2 3 4 5	
Topic transitions, tie-ins, summaries, analogies	1 2 3 4 5	
Interaction with class participants	1 2 3 4 5	
Additional comments:		

Assessment Instruments

Having recently been promoted to management, Deb was excited to attend her company's leadership academy. The series of seminars was designed to provide her with all of the information she would need to be an effective sales manager. Course topics included hiring staff, establishing performance expectations, giving effective feedback, conducting performance reviews, and understanding corporate tools and resources. The final session was scheduled to be via teleconference so that the new managers could work from their own desks, allowing them to search for and use various corporate online management resources.

Three weeks prior to the first training session, Deb received a packet of pre-work materials in inter-office mail. In addition to two articles that she was to read prior to the class, she received information about a 360-degree feedback instrument. She wasn't familiar with 360-degree feedback, so she read the associated materials with great care.

Deb learned that 360-degree feedback was a tool that would allow her to assess her own leadership style and skills while also receiving feedback from her supervisor and from the staff who report to her. The feedback instrument that her company used was processed online. She was provided with instructions about how to choose which of her employees to provide her feedback and how to introduce the concept of 360-degree feedback to the people who would rate her.

The concept seemed intriguing, but also a bit frightening. She was prepared to give feedback to her employees, but was unsure whether she wanted her employees to give feedback to her. Nonetheless, she sent out the information, along with the links to the feedback instrument, and she asked her subordinates and supervisor to rate her.

When the first class session was held, all of the participants had their 360-degree feedback reports awaiting them. The instructor walked them through the reports and explained how to interpret the data and, more importantly, how to use the information to help improve their leadership skills.

To Deb's surprise, she learned a great deal about how her boss and her employees perceived her, and she was able to use this information to set some goals for herself. As the other leadership classes were held, she paid special attention to the particular modules that focused on the skill areas where she had scored low.

Back on the job, Deb acknowledged to the respondents that she learned a lot about herself through the 360-degree assessment, and she indicated which areas she was going to work on developing.

What Is an Assessment Instrument?

Simply put, an assessment instrument is a tool designed to solicit and communicate information about an individual, team, or organization. Some of the instruments also provide an analysis of the results, along with feedback or developmental suggestions. While merely completing an assessment is an activity, the analysis, feedback, and development features cause us to include assessments as a training solution. Assessment instruments can be in paper-and-pencil form or available via computer. Paper-and-pencil assessments require a manual tabulation of results, while most of the online instruments have the built-in capacity to tabulate and analyze results. Assessment instruments may ask only the individual to respond, or they can be multi-rater assessments (MRA), where additional respondents are asked to rate an individual's skills or style.

Some of the more common types of assessment instruments measure:

- Career development
- Change readiness
- Communication style
- Conflict management approach
- General training needs
- Leadership development needs
- Learning style
- Management style
- Personality type
- 360-degree feedback
- Team effectiveness
- Topic knowledge
- Training needs

Assessments can be of great benefit when added to an organization's toolkit of training solutions. They can provide rich information to the trainer and to the participants about their current knowledge or skill levels. They are not, however, without some downsides. Some pros and cons are listed below.

Pros

- Can provide timely feedback;
- Can provide instant answers to skill questions, letting learners know immediately whether they answered questions incorrectly;
- Can be used to collect training needs information and may also track skill gap closure (the measure between what level of skill is needed and what level of skill an employee actually has); and

- Reach across geographic areas, as both paper-and-pencil and computerized assessments can be used in a global environment.

Cons

- Negative results can be demoralizing for learners;

- Responses may not be received on time;

- Those responding to online instruments can have security concerns, so you must ensure that recipients cannot gain access to individual answers or view others' responses or results;

- They aren't useful if recipients don't act on the feedback received;

- They aren't practical for all subject areas;

- They can be misused by management; and

- They can be expensive to buy, and development of customized assessment tools may be cost prohibitive.

When to Use Assessments

Assessment instruments are most helpful when you want to gather information about individuals, teams, or organizations. While some provide more valid data than others, in general, they are designed to gather unbiased, realistic, and timely information—often from a variety of sources. Use them to assess organizational learning needs, effectiveness in teams, and styles or skills possessed by your employees. Assessment instruments are most effective in organizations when anonymity of responses can be ensured and when the organization is committed to using assessments for developmental purposes.

How to Implement Assessments

Using assessment instruments can be as simple as including one in a classroom training session or as complex as administering one to all employees in a worldwide company. As always, complete a needs assessment as a first step to ensure that the assessment instrument meets the intended goals and objectives. Then follow these steps:

1. Select the appropriate instrument for the need.

2. Administer the assessment instrument.

3. Analyze the data.

4. Communicate the results and develop action plans.

1. Select the Appropriate Instrument for the Need

A wide variety of assessment instruments have been developed and are available commercially. In determining which assessment instrument to use, consider the following:

- The skill or style to be assessed;

- Readiness for feedback;

- Availability of respondents;

- Literacy level;

- Credibility of the instrument; and

- Design of feedback reports.

The Skill or Style to Be Assessed. The first consideration is to define clearly what information you are seeking. An assessment instrument that provides feedback on a manager's knowledge of how to supervise is quite different from one that assesses his or her behavior as a manager. Your training goals and objectives will help you determine what type of assessment is most appropriate.

Readiness for Feedback. Consider your recipients and their willingness to accept and act on feedback before using an assessment tool. If learners are fearful that any feedback collected may be used against them, they may hesitate to ask for feedback or may select only those respondents they feel will give them positive feedback, which may defeat the purpose.

Availability of Respondents. Availability is a key consideration when using multi-rater feedback assessment instruments. If your organization is implementing a 360-degree feedback program and all managers send their assessments to all of their peers at the same time, it's possible that each manager will be asked to evaluate a dozen or more other managers, all within a limited time frame. This may negatively impact the number of responses received or the thought put into them.

When implementing assessments, it's important to communicate why the assessment is being done, whether or not the responses are confidential, and what will be done with the data. All of these steps will help ensure that respondents do indeed complete a request for feedback.

Literacy Level. Consideration should be given to the literacy level of both the recipient and the respondents. If an online instrument is used, make sure that respondents all have access to computers and know how to respond. As with printed materials, it's important that the questions be written at or below the education level of those responding to the assessment. A general rule of thumb is to select instruments that are written at a seventh-grade level to ensure that most, if not all, employees are able to read and respond to the questions appropriately.

Credibility of the Instrument. In some organizations, using assessments that are research-based and are proven to be both valid and reliable is of utmost importance to the recipients. In other organizations, using a tool that is familiar is of greater value. In selecting assessment instruments, you must know what is important to the members of your organization.

Design of Feedback Reports. No assessment is of value to your organization if the feedback data is not organized in an easy-to-understand format. When choosing between different instruments that measure the same data, the design of the feedback report may be the tiebreaker. Reports with graphs and color tend to be easier to read. Reports with a lot of detail may be preferred by an organization filled with technical people.

Once all of these factors have been considered, you are ready to select your instrument. Several of the more common assessment instruments are listed at the end of this chapter, along with contact information. This listing is not an endorsement of any of them, but is intended simply as an aid for you in beginning your search. Remember that not all instruments are created equally; if you choose to purchase a pre-developed one, be sure to investigate the reputation of the developing company as well as the quality of the instrument itself.

2. Administer the Assessment Instrument

It is important to administer any instrument with a minimum of bias. Most instruments include specific administration guidelines; you will be most effective if you follow these guidelines closely and don't attempt to provide any additional directions or explanations. When using an assessment instrument for the first time, be clear with participants about the purpose of the instrument, confidentiality, and how the results will be used. Respondents will be hesitant to provide honest feedback if they feel their responses won't be kept confidential. You can alleviate these concerns by having an outside party administer the assessment instrument.

3. Analyze the Data

Determine whether you will perform the analysis or if the recipients of the feedback will analyze their own results. Most assessment instruments include analysis instructions as part of the package. Online instruments frequently include some level of analysis as a part of the purchase price.

4. Communicate the Results and Develop Action Plans

Once the instrument has been administered and results have been calculated and analyzed, the information has to be communicated to the recipient. A clear and thorough explanation of the results will help recipients be able to use the feedback to develop their skills. If you communicate the results in a classroom setting, be careful to ensure that each recipient sees only his or her own results.

Even when the feedback is positive, recipients tend to experience some common reactions. They typically move through four stages, called the SARA model: surprise, anger, rejection, and acceptance. Some spend more time than others in some or all of the phases, but they generally do move through all four in the order described below.

- *Surprise*—It is common for recipients to be surprised by the feedback that comes from their peers or others. The recipient may expect either more positive or less positive opinions from co-workers.

- *Anger*—This reaction is more common when the feedback received is negative. Recipients would like their co-workers to think more highly of them than they think of themselves. Even when the respondent's perception matches the individual's perception, resentment is quite possible.

- *Rejection*—It is normal for those receiving feedback to want to refute it. Common responses include, "They don't really know me," or "I selected the wrong people to give me feedback." As with anger, this is most common with negative feedback. However, even positive feedback can be rejected; for example, one manager who received high scores on encouraging diversity rejected the feedback because she felt she didn't do enough to promote diversity in the organization.

- *Acceptance*—Once the other three stages are moved through, the recipient is ready to accept the feedback and to act on it. This stage can come quickly, or it may take a great deal of time. The recipients must get to this stage before he or she will be able to effectively do anything with the feedback received.

Typically, you will ask the learners to plan some actions as a result of the feedback they receive. Allow time in class for the learners to absorb the feedback and to create action plans. You may want to follow up with participants a few months after the session to ensure they are using the feedback to their benefit.

How to Blend Assessments with Classroom Training

Blending assessment instruments with classroom training can be a highly effective combination for achieving an overall training goal. As will be discussed further in Chapter 14, "Job Aids," the assessment instruments should have a similar look or be formatted the same as the other classroom materials, if at all possible. In general, you can use the instruments before, during, or after a classroom session.

Before the Session

Assessment instruments are commonly administered prior to a classroom session when completing a needs analysis or in preparation for classroom content (for example, assessing the participants' own learning styles in preparation for a train-the-trainer class). They can also be enormously helpful for gathering information when doing a gap analysis or when collecting data to determine specific learning objectives. (See Chapter 3, "Determine the Need," for more information about using assessment instruments for needs analysis or about conducting needs analyses in general.) When you are using an assessment instrument in preparation for a classroom session, send the participants the instrument and associated instructions in advance and ask them to return the results to you by a designated deadline. Be sure to explain the purpose of the instrument and discuss confidentiality of results. In organizations where confidentiality is a concern, you may not want to introduce assessment instruments prior to a classroom session.

During the Session

Administer assessment instruments during the session itself when you don't know your participants in advance, when the schedule doesn't allow for it to be administered in advance, or when you suspect there would be a low return rate from the participants. You can also use instruments to provide an alternative learning method and to provide interest and variation. When administering assessment instruments during the session, keep in mind that many people experience anxiety when taking anything resembling a test, so offer reassurances if necessary. We recommend administering an assessment instrument right before a break so any stragglers don't feel pressured to complete theirs in order for the session to continue. Assessment instruments such as 360-degree feedback may be introduced in the classroom session, with respondents actually completing the instrument outside of the classroom. (In Exhibits 11.1 and 11.2 at the end of the chapter, we provide a list of tips for choosing respondents and a template for requesting feedback from others. These can be given to your learners.)

Once you've analyzed each returned instrument, you can share the results with the participants as an activity or in support of related content. Keep in mind that people often prize their privacy and only share individuals' results if the situation and the content warrant doing so—and then only after receiving permission from all of the learners.

After the Session

Filling out assessment instruments after a classroom session is usually done as part of an evaluation process. You can either distribute them at the end of the session or send them afterward with a request to return them to you by a designated deadline. In these situations, the assessment tool can serve both as a measure of learning that occurred in the classroom and as a reinforcement of the material covered in class. A post-test, for example, may cause the learner to review the course content prior to completing the assessment, which in turn reinforces the content that was taught.

Some common examples of blending assessments with classroom training include:

- The use of 360-degree feedback instruments prior to a management development program;

- Administration of a communication style assessment during a communication class; and

- Conducting an assessment of learning at the completion of safety training.

Exhibits 11.3 and 11.4 are samples of assessment instruments. See Chapters 5 through 7 for additional information on how to blend training solutions.

KEY POINTS

- Assessment instruments may be effectively used before, during, or after training.

- Carefully select from the numerous assessment instruments that are available to ensure you use a tool that is appropriate for your organization's learning needs.

- Clearly explain to your learners why and how assessment instruments will be used.

- Encourage your learners to use the data from the assessment instruments to enhance their performance.

RESOURCES

The following listing is not an endorsement of any of these tools, but is intended simply as an aid for you in beginning your search. Remember that not all instruments are created equally; if you choose to purchase a pre-developed one, be sure to investigate the reputation of the developing company, as well as the quality of the instrument itself.

Career Development

- *Career beliefs inventory* (CBI). CPP, Inc. (800) 624-1765. [www.cpp.com].

- *Strong interest inventory*. CPP, Inc. (800) 624-1765. [www.cpp.com].

Change Readiness

- Maurer, R. (1996). *Beyond the wall of resistance: Unconventional strategies that build support for change*. Austin, TX: Bard Press.

Communication Styles

- *Influence styles inventory questionnaire* (ISI). HRD Press. (800) 822-2801. [www.hrdpress.com].

- *Myers-Briggs type instrument*. CPP, Inc. (800) 624-1765. [www.cpp.com].

Conflict Management

- *Thomas-Kilmann conflict mode instrument* (TKI). CPP, Inc. (800) 624-1765. [www.cpp.com].

General Assessment Information

- Burn, B., & Payment, M. (2000) *Assessments A – Z: A collection of 50 questionnaires, instruments, and inventories (*with CD-ROM). San Francisco, CA: Jossey-Bass.

Leadership Style/Development Needs

- Blake R., & Mouton, J. (1978). *The new managerial grid*. Houston, TX: Gulf.

- *Leadership development needs analysis*. Trainers Direct. (800) 250-1570. [www.trainersdirect.com].

- *Leadership practices inventory* (LPI). Kouzes & Posner. (877) 762-2974. [www.lpionline.com/lpi/].

Learning Styles

- *A self-portrait™ learning style profile reflective educational perspectives*. (805) 648-1739. [www.redp.com].

- *Learning style questionnaire*. HRD Press. (800) 822-2801. [www.hrdpress.com].

Management Styles

- *Emotional intelligence appraisal*. TalentSmart. (888) 818-SMART. [www.talentsmart.com].

- *Management training development needs analysis*. Trainers Direct. (800) 250-1570. [www.trainersdirect.com].

Personality Types

- *Disc classic*. Mills and Associates. (888) 662-2424. [www.discprofile.com].

- *Myers-Briggs type instrument*. CPP, Inc. (800) 624-1765. [www.cpp.com].

Team Effectiveness

- *Insights discovery team effectiveness diagnostic®*. Insights Learning & Development. [www.insightsworld.com].

- *Team performance questionnaire*. *Team Development Workbook*. Jossey-Bass. (877) 762-2974. [www.josseybass.com].

360-Degree Feedback

- *Clark Wilson Group*. (800) 537-7249. [www. cwginc.com].

- *Leadership Mirror*. DDI. (800) 933-4463. [www.ddiworld.com].

Training Ability

- *Instructor development needs analysis*. Trainers Direct. (800) 250-1570. [www.trainersdirect.com].

Training Needs Analysis

- *Staff training needs analysis*. Trainers Direct. (800) 250-1570. [www.trainersdirect.com].

- *Training and educational leader self-assessment* (TELSA). Trainers Direct. (800) 250-1570. [www.trainersdirect.com].

- *Training program self-assessment tool*. Trainers Direct. (800) 250-1570. [www.trainersdirect.com].

Exhibit 11.1. Tips on Choosing Respondents to a 360-Degree Survey.

- Select individuals who know your work—people with whom you interact frequently.
- Choose people you have worked with for at least six months.
- Select a mix of respondents; choose people you work well with, as well as people who are more of a challenge for you.
- Be sure to let respondents know that their responses will be combined with those of the other respondents, so that no individual answers or comments can be attributed to any specific person.
- Select people who are most likely to provide you with candid feedback.

Exhibit 11.2. Sample Letter for Introducing 360-Degree Feedback to Respondents.

Dear [Name]:

I am participating in a management development class. As part of the class, I will be working to improve my management skills. But first, I need to learn about my current management style. To help me with this, I am asking you to please complete the attached management style assessment instrument.

This questionnaire will take you only about twenty minutes to complete. Your answers will be confidential, so please be completely honest. All answers are being sent to the instructor for tabulation, and I will not see any of the individual completed assessment forms.

Please complete the instrument and return it to [instructor's name] at [instructor's address] by [date].

I appreciate your willingness to help me further develop my management skills. If you have any questions or concerns, please give me a call.

Sincerely,

[Your Name]

Exhibit 11.3. Sample Assessment Instrument 1.

Organizational Skills

Do you know enough about organizing your workspace? Organized workspaces don't happen because of magic. They are the result of plans—and efforts to maintain those plans. Take the following assessment to discover how many helpful techniques and work habits you use to organize your workspace.

Instructions: Rate yourself on each of the techniques and work habits listed below according to the following scale.

1 = Rarely or never; 2 = Sometimes; 3 = Almost always

_____ 1. I clear off my work area at the end of each workday.

_____ 2. I have a designated place for incoming materials and I use it.

_____ 3. I have a designated place for unread mail and I use it.

_____ 4. I have a designated place for professional material that I want to read later.

_____ 5. I handle each piece of my incoming mail only once.

_____ 6. I keep clutter off my work area.

_____ 7. I have a system for managing my incoming e-mail messages and I use it.

_____ 8. I use color-coding to help with paper filing.

_____ 9. I maintain a file that reminds me of important items for follow-up.

_____ 10. I can find information from my files within two attempts.

_____ 11. I have a daily "to do" list and I use it.

_____ 12. I have a list of current projects, which I consult and update frequently.

_____ 13. I clean out my files on a regular basis.

_____ 14. I use a system for keeping track of contact information.

_____ 15. My workspace is neat and orderly at all times.

_____ Total

Exhibit 11.3. Sample Assessment Instrument 1, *Continued*.

Scoring and Interpretation

Instructions: Total your responses and put the number on the line following the statements. Although no one is perfectly organized at all times, if your score is above 35 you appear to others to be well-organized. You know it takes some work to get that way and stay that way. You could probably teach your co-workers a few tips and tricks you have learned that will help them. Congratulations to you for having an organized workspace and good organizing habits.

If your score is 29 to 34, you have some good organizing habits and ideas. You probably become too busy or distracted to do a better job of organizing your workspace. You know being organized helps make your work life easier, so set aside time to make an organization plan.

If your score is below 29, you have difficulty keeping track of important information and events. You probably miss important dates. You likely spend time apologizing to your co-workers for your disorganization. The good news is that you can improve your situation by learning and practicing new skills immediately.

Exhibit 11.4. Sample Assessment Instrument 2.

Rewards and Recognition

How can you reward and recognize your team members? It's not possible to receive too much appreciation! Your teammates are more likely to feel they are not appreciated enough. It is time to change that! Learn ways to express your appreciation from the following assessment.

Instructions: After the following numbers, list as many ways as you can think of to reward and recognize your team members. It may help to think of individual team members for inspiration, or you may think of all the ways you would like to be rewarded and recognized by others. Go for quantity of ideas, not quality.

1.

2.

3.

4.

5.

6.

7.

8.

Exhibit 11.4. Sample Assessment Instrument 2, *Continued.*

9.

10.

11.

12.

13.

14.

15.

16.

Scoring and Interpretation

Instructions: If you have completed this assessment in a team situation, circle the one item that is especially appealing to you as a way to be rewarded or recognized. Put your name on your list and pass it around to your teammates, who will do the same. Read the lists you receive. On a separate sheet of paper, make notes for yourself of what types of rewards and recognition your teammates prefer. In the future you will be able to use these ideas to recognize others.

12

Instructor-Led e-Learning

John knew he should take more advantage of technology to train employees, but just didn't have the time to figure it all out. When he was honest with himself, he admitted he didn't really have the interest either; he felt intimidated by the very idea and didn't want to admit to any technical person how little he knew. He managed to avoid even discussing the issue until one day when he and his friend Mary were talking about how much e-mail had changed the way they did their day-to-day jobs. Both remembered the days before e-mail—when they wasted huge amounts of time playing telephone tag just to get answers to questions, spent hours trying to schedule training sessions, and had to print out and send material through inter-office mail or even the post office. John was greatly surprised when his friend mentioned how often she used e-mail in her e-learning activities. *E-mail* is e-learning? "Sure, it's one of the e-learning techniques," she replied. "I use it often to introduce material before people come to a classroom session, and even more often after classes to remind people of what they learned and to encourage them to practice the techniques and methods covered in the session." "Well," thought John, "if that's what e-learning is, maybe even I can begin to use it."

The next time he and Mary talked, he asked her about other e-learning techniques she used. She mentioned chat rooms, which she scheduled following her project management classes. The participants met each week in a chat room to discuss how they had applied the techniques learned in class, what worked, and what didn't and to use each other as sounding boards for issues raised on their current projects. Mary also told John about her current software training classes, which she was delivering to remote sites using online presentation software. He was too embarrassed to ask her what she meant and was relieved when she invited him to sit in on her next class. He received an invitation via e-mail that explained how to join the online class using his personal computer and office telephone. Mary spent the first few minutes of the class explaining how online classes worked; by the end of the session, John was pleased that he could see how to use the company's new TruLux software, hear the questions from participants in three different countries, and even practice on the new software, all without leaving his own desk. "Well," he thought again, "this is MUCH easier than traveling to Pittsburgh for the quarterly update classes—maybe I can do this after all!"

What Is Instructor-Led e-Learning?

E-learning is any training technique where the primary delivery method is electronic and content is delivered via the Internet, intranet/extranet, audio or video technology, and/or CD-ROM. We distinguish between two types of e-learning: instructor-led and self-study. In this chapter, we'll discuss instructor-led e-learning solutions (also known as synchronous e-learning), including webinars, teleconferencing, videoconferencing, chat rooms, bulletin boards, and e-mail.

In this chapter we outline how to use each of these methods to enhance the content learned in a classroom as well as to encourage the participants to transfer the learning into changes in their behavior back on the job.

Webinars

A webinar is an instructor-led online training session where the trainer uses software such as NetMeeting®, WebEx®, or Placeware® to share electronic information of all kinds (word processing documents, web pages, applications, or presentation software such as Microsoft PowerPoint®). The participants can sit at their own desks, see the material being presented on their own PCs, and talk with the trainer and other participants over the telephone or via e-mail. This type of training can be particularly effective in introducing new software or with any content that can be depicted visually and discussed in group settings. Webinars can be enormously helpful for delivering training to people scattered geographically.

Teleconferencing

Teleconferencing is using the telephone to deliver training. An instructor leads the session and often enhances the delivery by sending handouts and/or PowerPoint® presentations in advance so that participants can follow along during the call. Specialized telephone lines are used to provide access to a large number of participants; these are commonly referred to as bridge lines. As with webinars, teleconferencing can be helpful for delivering training to people scattered geographically and across a wide variety of time zones.

Videoconferencing

Videoconferencing is similar to teleconferencing, but with the addition of participants being able to see one another on TV monitors. Videoconferencing requires that the trainers and all participants have access to specialized equipment; if the company doesn't have the equipment in-house, commercial businesses such as Kinko's lease videoconferencing services. This equipment may include TV monitors, cameras, and audio equipment, as well as the cabling necessary to transmit the signals to and from all of the locations.

Chat Rooms

Chat rooms are online versions of discussion groups and can be used for any content that could benefit from participants sharing experiences, asking questions, and/or solving problems. Chat "rooms" are located on a website, where people communicate with each other in "real time" by typing messages that show up immediately (or almost immediately) on the screens of the others in the chat room. Chat rooms are similar to teleconferencing, except the discussion is done via computer rather than telephone.

Bulletin Boards

Bulletin boards—also known as forums or discussions—are similar to chat rooms in that all "conversation" between people is sent and received by typing messages and sending them through the Internet. The difference between the two is that of timing; chat rooms allow people to communicate in "real time," much like verbal conversations. Bulletin boards, on the other hand, are started by the instructor posting a question, to which the participants respond at their convenience, creating a "thread" of responses (a sample is included in Exhibit 12.1 at the end of this chapter). Bulletin boards are useful in that they allow the participants to respond at their convenience. Unlike chat rooms, they allow the learners time to think through how they wish to respond after reading the question and others' replies.

Using a bulletin board for an online discussion can provide a significant step toward moving the participants' classroom learning into actual behavioral change. It's an economical method (time-wise and travel-wise) for bringing classroom participants back together to review material, ask questions of the instructor and each other, and obtain support and feedback for attempts they've made in trying out the new behaviors.

E-Mail

E-mail is basically an electronic form of letter writing. However, unlike writing letters and sending information the old-fashioned way, e-mail allows us to send multiple copies of the same information to large numbers of people and to expect a delivery time of minutes or even seconds, as opposed to days or weeks. Delivery can often be scheduled for a specific day (or even hour, depending on the software), and it is particularly helpful in communicating with participants before classroom sessions take place and for sharing reminders and/or new information afterward.

Some pros and cons of instructor-led e-learning are listed below. Also see Exhibit 12.2 at the end of the chapter for samples of using e-mail for e-learning.

Pros

- Can be relatively easy to implement (for example, by using e-mail and chat rooms);

- Often doesn't require much development time;

- Provides almost instant feedback opportunities;

- Can be effective and efficient for employees in different locations and time zones; and

- Provides flexibility for learners to attend training from a location convenient to them.

Cons

- Can be overlooked by busy employees;

- Requires a certain level of computer literacy;

- Can require specialized equipment and/or software;

- Requires unique trainer skills (both technical skills and—except for videoconferencing—the ability to keep learners engaged without using or seeing body language); and

- Doesn't provide in-person contact between instructors and participants.

When to Use Instructor-Led e-Learning

Generally speaking, instructor-led e-learning solutions are appropriate when the intended audience members (1) are comfortable with technology; (2) are dispersed geographically; and (3) work a variety of time shifts (e-mail in particular works well).

Comfortable with Technology. If the members of your intended audience are not comfortable with using the technology, the solutions you choose may not be used effectively. You can still choose to implement them; just keep in mind that you may need to overcome resistance, provide education on e-learning benefits, and even supply training on the technology itself before your participants will fully benefit from the training.

Dispersed Geographically. Using instructor-led e-learning solutions can be effective when working with employees who are located in far-flung locations. This is especially true if only a few people work at each location; in this case, using teleconferencing and webinars, for example, could provide effective training without incurring significant travel expenses.

Work a Variety of Time Shifts. When you have learners working a variety of schedules, getting them together can be a daunting task. Instructor-led e-learning offers more flexibility than other training solutions; e-mail and bulletin boards in particular can be used to provide ongoing training reminders, review, and/or discussions without the need for scheduling at all. Webinars, teleconferencing, and videoconferencing still require scheduling, but offer greater flexibility than other instructor-led solutions.

How to Implement Instructor-Led e-Learning

Using e-learning solutions to augment classroom training is most successful with participants who are comfortable and skilled at using technology. If you attempt to use e-learning with people who are unskilled or even frightened by technology, you often spend so much time teaching them how to use the programs that they don't have time to learn the training content. Technology is so all-persuasive in our culture today that this is easy to overlook; but the reality is that, even today, some employees lack even the most basic computer skills.

How to Implement Webinars

The skills needed for delivering webinars include expertise in running the online software itself, the ability to keep learners engaged and focused while they're sitting at their own desks, and the knack of reading the mood of the participants without the benefit of body language.

We highly recommend practicing with the software before your first training session, even the more simple-to-use ones, or if you're using familiar software in a new setting. Technology is so interdependent on network and computer settings that what worked one way in one setting may not work the same way in another setting or may not work at all. Participants are generally unforgiving when someone has technical difficulties; since they can't see you, they don't empathize with you as much as they do when you're physically present. Follow these tips when using webinars to augment your training program:

1. Prepare for delivery.

2. Keep the sessions short.

3. Use the interactive features of the software for evaluation.

4. Expect to spend extra time initially teaching participants how to use the technology.

1. Prepare for Delivery. Any training is more likely to be successful if you're well-prepared, but with online presentations, it's critical. Because you can't see the participants (and they can't see you), maintaining their interest is much more difficult. If you need to spend even ninety seconds locating the document you wish to share, you may have lost a participant's attention for an entire hour-long session. For one thing, participants are often sitting at their own desks, surrounded by their current job responsibilities, and are very easily distracted. A co-worker stopping by, an e-mail notice popping up, or a phone ringing may be enough to remove a participant completely from your training and take him or her back into the pressures of ongoing responsibilities. Materials should be visually engaging for online presentations. Also consider preparing question-and-answer sections and polling or testing to ensure that participants remain interested.

2. Keep the Sessions Short. Sitting in front of a computer while listening on a conference call is physically more exhausting for most learners than sitting in a classroom, especially if they are holding phones to their ears instead of using headsets. For this reason, you'll be more successful if you keep your sessions short, generally an hour or so in length. If you have more content than can be covered in a short session, it's generally more effective to schedule a series of hour-long sessions than it is to include all of the content in a single sitting.

3. **Use the Interactive Features of the Software for Evaluation.** Most online presentation programs contain some form of "polling" that can be used for evaluation. WebEx®, for example, contains the capacity to check for learning on the spot through the use of spontaneous or previously prepared Level 2 evaluation tests. You can choose to share the results of the test with the participants or not, and you can choose to save the results for later review. You can also view the results as a group score or see the results of an individual participant. Polling can also be used for Level 1 evaluation to determine how well the participants liked the course content, your delivery, and/or the use of the online presentation software itself. Review Chapter 8, "Measure the Results of the Program," for more information on evaluation levels.

4. **Expect to Spend Extra Time Initially Teaching Participants How to Use the Technology.** If your participants have never used online presentation software, you will inevitably spend the first few minutes (sometimes as many as fifteen or twenty) waiting for people to find the e-mail invitation, navigate to the meeting site, and complete the process of logging into the meeting itself. Rather than starting immediately with your content, we recommend spending those minutes briefly reviewing basic instructions for the online presentation software itself (for example, the components of the meeting window, using "chat" capability, responding to polls, raising one's "hand" to ask questions). Whatever content you cover during these first few minutes, you'll likely be doing so in between participants' how-do-I-join-the-meeting questions. As your participants get used to this type of training, the time spent at the beginning tends to become shorter and shorter.

How to Implement Teleconferencing

Teleconferencing can be extremely easy to implement. Follow the tips below to make your teleconference training sessions most effective:

1. Keep the sessions short.

2. Start with introductions.

3. Review ground rules.

4. Send e-mail reminders.

5. Facilitate the session.

1. Keep the Sessions Short. Talking and listening on a telephone can be physically exhausting, especially if the participants are using a handheld telephone rather than a headset. They also may lose interest quickly because they don't have any visual stimulation, unless you provide handouts and/or an online software presentation. For these reasons, keep your teleconferencing sessions to a maximum of an hour in length, just as with webinars. If you need to spend more time to cover all of your content, schedule a series of shorter sessions rather than trying to cover all of the information in a single session.

2. Start with Introductions. As with webinars, none of the teleconferencing participants can see each other, so introductions are very important. We recommend that you start each session with very brief introductions, asking people to provide their names and one other item, such as from where they're calling.

3. Review Ground Rules. One way to make your teleconferences more successful is to establish ground rules at the beginning of each class. These ground rules might include items such as:

- Start every question or comment with your name, for example, "Hi, this is Ellen, and I have a quick question about the material you just covered."

- Use the mute button on your telephone when you're not actually speaking—to minimize extraneous noise.

- Don't come late or leave early, or if you must, be sure to let the instructor know in advance.

4. Send e-Mail Reminders. Send an e-mail reminder of the teleconference to participants and include the date, time, teleconference call-in number, and access code (password). If you have time, send two (one a week before, another the day before). For some reason, people tend to need more reminders of training sessions if they don't physically have to leave their work areas to attend. They'll appreciate the reminders, and you'll be more likely to have full attendance.

5. Facilitate the Session. Using a teleconference for training may be new to participants, and you may have to actively encourage them to participate. Keep each presentation of new information short (ideally five to seven minutes), and follow each one with prepared discussion questions. Allow time for the participants to respond, even if the silence can initially be unnerving. Calling on participants by name will prevent people talking over one another, although be aware that some people will find this practice alarming and may feel "put on the spot." Use this technique when you're fairly certain the participants have developed feelings of comfort and trust.

How to Implement Videoconferencing

Videoconferencing can be used in much the same way as classroom training, without the need for the learners and instructor to be physically together. With videoconferencing, participants in different locations can see and hear each other and view the instructor, who can use lectures, presentation software, demonstrations, and even discussions in much the same way as he or she would if everyone were in the same room together. Keep in mind that visibility is somewhat diminished and prepare all materials accordingly. Sometimes you'll also notice a small video or audio transmission delay when the sites are connected using slow transmission speeds, which can result in people at multiple sites starting to speak at the same time. To accommodate this delay, allow a few seconds for people at other locations to ask or respond to a question. Using videoconferencing rather than webinars allows you to see the reactions of the participants.

Videoconferencing involves four basic steps: (1) prepare; (2) begin the session; (3) keep it interactive; and (4) wrap up.

1. Prepare. Your first step is to reserve the videoconference facilities and an operator, if needed. Be sure to notify participants of the day, time, location, and any dial-in codes (for the audio portion of the session), remembering to take time zone differences into consideration. You or your operator will want to arrive early to test the equipment prior to the session. Because a remote site may already have called into your videoconferencing system, assume someone can see and hear you the minute you step into the room. It's also a good idea to have a wall clock hanging behind the camera so that you can easily keep track of the time.

2. Begin the Session. Welcome the participants once all of the sites have been connected. Always begin with a roll call to acquaint participants with speaking in the videoconferencing setting and to introduce them to one another. Encourage participants to respond and to ask questions, but communicate the protocol for doing so (Will you routinely call on each location or take questions as they occur?).

Each site will have microphones or speakerphones in order to transmit audio. Remind participants to speak clearly and concisely so all can hear. To cut down on distracting noises, ask that people mute their microphones when they are not talking.

3. Keep It Interactive. The advantage offered by a videoconference is the ability to be highly interactive, not just be a "talking head." Design your teleconference training session to include opportunities for interaction. For example, you might ask people at each site one at a time whether anyone there has questions, thoughts, or ideas and then wait for them to respond. Standard classroom training practices are equally useful during a videoconference. For example, change the activity or pace every twenty minutes, be alert for signs of low energy, and take a break if participant liveliness appears to be diminishing.

4. Wrap Up. When you've covered all of your subject matter and met your training objectives, it's time to wrap up the session. Allot a few minutes at the end to summarize, be sure all questions have been answered, and be sure to allow time for an evaluation. An evaluation form can be sent to participants, or you can conduct a verbal evaluation during the videoconference itself.

How to Implement Chat Rooms

Chat rooms can be set up through various websites on the Internet. The skills required to successfully use chat rooms are similar to those for any online learning program and include expertise in the technology itself, the ability to keep learners engaged and focused while they're sitting at their own desks, and the knack of reading the mood of the participants without the benefit of body language or even voice cues. Keep the following things in mind when using chat rooms for learning purposes:

1. Schedule the chat room discussion(s) in advance.

2. Encourage participants new to chat rooms to practice.

3. Send e-mail reminders.

4. Facilitate the discussion.

1. Schedule the Chat Room Discussion(s) in Advance. Arrange the schedule for the chat room either prior to or during the classroom session. Because technology is intimidating to many people, your participants may decide that it's easier to not show up for the chat room discussion. To place them at ease, spend at least a few minutes during the classroom session demonstrating how to use chat rooms, explaining their intended purpose and benefits, and answering questions for those who may be new to the idea.

2. Encourage Participants New to Chat Rooms to Practice. If your participants are new to chat rooms, encourage them to participate in one prior to participating in yours. Be prepared to share a few sample chat rooms on topics you think may be of interest to your audience, and let them know they can "lurk" in a chat room without joining in the discussion until they feel comfortable doing so. Encourage them to read books and/or visit websites on "netiquette" (online etiquette) and provide a listing of your favorites to make it easy for them to do so. We've included a few netiquette websites in the Resources section at the end of this chapter.

3. Send e-Mail Reminders. Send an e-mail reminder about the chat room discussion to participants; it can be a brief statement of date, time, and place. If you have time, send two (one a week before, another the day before). Be sure to include the link or provide the website for the chat room site. You can also include a brief reminder statement of the topic to be discussed and encourage the participants to review or research it in advance (if appropriate).

4. Facilitate the Discussion. During the chat itself, be prepared to facilitate the discussion, yet allow a certain freedom for spontaneous questions and comments. As with in-person discussions, chat rooms can range from very formal to wild brainstorming melees, and, as with in-person discussions, it's your job as the facilitator to set and maintain the tone of the conversation. You can choose to come prepared with specific discussion questions based on the subject matter or allow the participants' questions and feedback to determine the course of the discussion. We recommend that you come equipped with at least a few prepared questions; as with in-person discussions, sometimes you need to "prime the pump" in order to get people to start actively participating.

How to Implement Bulletin Boards

Use bulletin boards before the training session to encourage participants to introduce themselves or their experience with the topic or afterward to provide discussion questions for material introduced during a classroom session. When implementing bulletin boards, follow these tips:

1. Prepare for the discussion.

2. Expect to spend extra time initially teaching participants how to use the technology.

3. Explain your expectations of the bulletin board's use during the classroom session.

4. Actively participate in the discussion.

1. Prepare for the Discussion. As are the other instructor-led e-learning options, bulletin boards are an excellent way to facilitate discussions among instructors and participants without requiring them to be physically together. Bulletin boards are unique in that they allow participants time to more carefully prepare their responses. For this reason, select and prepare discussion questions that have enough "meat" to keep a prolonged discussion going and that will allow the participants to respond with examples from their own workplaces or personal lives.

The steps required to create questions within bulletin board software will vary depending on which software you use. However, most of the course management software applications (which include the bulletin board feature) listed at the end of the chapter include "wizards" that walk you through the mechanics of posting and updating bulletin board discussion questions.

2. **Expect to Spend Extra Time Initially Teaching Participants How to Use the Technology.** Bulletin boards—like many e-learning techniques—may be entirely new to many of your participants. Expect a few false starts when you introduce these techniques into your training program and spend enough time during the classroom session to at least verbally introduce participants to the steps involved in using this new method. You could also provide how-to instructions if necessary in the form of a job aid or through e-mail—and remember to include the website where you've posted the question. The most effective introduction to the technology would be through a hands-on classroom session where learners would actually log on to the bulletin board and practice using it, with an instructor there to help them if they need help.

3. **Explain Your Expectations of the Bulletin Board's Use During the Classroom Session.** Since your participants can respond to bulletin board discussion questions at their convenience, it's important that you clearly communicate the parameters of how and when they should respond. Will you expect them to use a more formal essay-writing format or the informal style used in e-mail? By what date do you expect them to respond? Do you want them to respond just to the discussion question or to others' responses as well?

4. **Actively Participate in the Discussion.** Actively participating in the discussion is the most effective way to make sure learners stay engaged and to intercept any misinformation before it spreads too far. You can also further spur discussion threads by adding comments to responses or by asking additional questions related to the original topic.

How to Implement e-Mail

E-mail is the easiest of e-learning tools to implement. It can be a powerful means to support classroom training, either before or after the classroom session actually occurs. Use e-mail before the training to welcome participants, to introduce them to new terminology, or to remind them to complete any course pre-work. Keep in mind that many people are overwhelmed by e-mail and may ignore yours, so be sure to clearly communicate when pre-work or post-work will be sent via e-mail, and include a clear description in the subject line so they recognize the e-mail immediately.

Use e-mail after the training session to deliver ongoing assignments, to remind people to use their newly acquired knowledge and skills, or to provide answers to questions that arose during class but you were unable to address, either because you didn't know the answer or didn't have the time to cover the topic. When using e-mail for learning purposes, keep in mind:

1. Keep the text of the message *very* short.

2. Announce and explain your e-mails during the classroom session.

3. Create distribution lists.

1. Keep the Text of the Message *Very* Short. People often fly through their e-mail boxes and may not read any message longer than six lines or so. This is especially true if they are not expecting the information. Keep the message to a minimum and feel free to not include any of the "niceties" you might normally insert into a written memo.

2. Announce and Explain Your e-Mails During the Classroom Session. Announce during the classroom session that you will be using e-mail as a follow-up to the class. Spend at least a few moments letting the participants know when you will be sending them, what topics you'll cover, and what their responses (if any) are expected to be.

3. Create Distribution Lists. A distribution list is an electronic grouping of e-mail addresses; we recommend that you create an e-mail distribution list if you're going to send more than one e-mail to the same group of people. You'll save yourself time and stress if you do so, and you will reduce the danger of inadvertently excluding a participant. You can create a distribution list using your e-mail program's capability or by simply copying all of the participants' e-mail addresses into a word processing document (separated by commas or semicolons) and then copying the list into the address line of your e-mail. Keep in mind that many people don't want their e-mail addresses shared, so send e-mails using the "blind copy" feature. This will ensure that no one receiving the e-mail can see any of the other recipients' e-mail addresses.

How to Blend Instructor-Led e-Learning with Classroom Training

As mentioned above, instructor-led e-learning can be used both prior to and following a classroom training session. You can schedule weekly chat room sessions, for example, to hold discussions about how well people are practicing the skills they learned in the classroom and to answer any questions that arise. Both teleconferencing and videoconferencing can be used for the same purpose, depending on the equipment available. Use webinars to present a short introduction of content material prior to the classroom session or as a way to review discussion points following it. Use a bulletin board to ask the participants to discuss a new management concept and how they've applied it in the workplace. Due to its common use, e-mail is the easiest solution to implement; use it to deliver introductory information to classroom participants before the training or to send weekly reminders and tips following it.

Examples of successful blending with classroom training include:

- Classroom training on effective supervisory skills, followed by a six-week series of hour-long online chats, videoconferences, or teleconferences designed to remind people of the new skills and to provide an opportunity for participants to discuss what has and has not worked for them.

- E-mails sent two weeks prior to classroom training on a company's new human resources policy. The e-mail text could include reminders of the classroom session's scheduled date and time, as well as instructions to read the attached documentation prior to attending the training.

- Short teleconferences, videoconferences, or chat rooms scheduled monthly to discuss how participants are using all the new features introduced in a new software training session.

- Basic written communication skills taught in a classroom session, followed by discussion questions posted on a bulletin board. This will encourage learners to review the content covered in class as well as practice their newly acquired skills.

- E-mail reminders and tips sent out weekly, reinforcing the new skills and knowledge learned in the new employee orientation training.

KEY POINTS

- Instructor-led e-learning solutions include online training, teleconferencing, videoconferencing, chat rooms, bulletin boards, and e-mail.

- These solutions offer training flexibility in terms of time and physical location when working with employees in far-flung work sites.

- Since these solutions are dependent on technology, they require specialized skills and equipment.

RESOURCES

Driscoll, M. (2002). *Web-based training: Designing e-learning experiences.* San Francisco, CA: Pfeiffer. Describes how to design web-based training programs and includes charts, tables, checklists, and a CD-ROM.

Horton, W., & Horton, K. (2003). *e-Learning tools and technologies: A consumer's guide for trainers, teachers, educators, and instructional designers.* Hoboken, NJ: John Wiley & Sons. A guide to identify, evaluate, and choose products and services based on different e-learning scenarios.

Shepard, S. (2002). *Videoconferencing demystified.* New York: McGraw-Hill. Describes what you need to know to use videoconferencing for meetings, training, or conferences; includes pros and cons, how to use components and equipment, and key technologies.

Spielman, S. (2003). *The web conferencing book: Understanding the technology, choose the right vendors, software, and equipment, start saving time and money today*. New York: AMACOM. Includes how to use web conferencing effectively, how to select appropriate vendors, software, and equipment, and why you would want to choose this technology.

WEBSITES

This listing contains websites that describe software that may assist you in designing and delivering instructor-led e-learning solutions. It is not an endorsement of any of the tools and services, but is intended simply as an aid for you in beginning your search.

Software
www.blackboard.com
www.desire2learn.com
www.embanet.com
www.microsoft.com/windows/netmeeting/.com
www.WebCT.com
www.webex.com

Netiquette
www.learnthenet.com
www.OnlineNetiquette.com

Exhibit 12.1. Sample Bulletin Board Discussion.

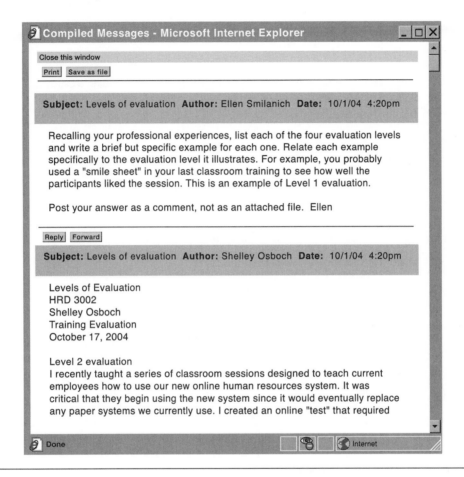

Exhibit 12.2. Sample e-Mails Pre- and Post-Class.

Pre-Classroom Sample

Greetings,

You are scheduled to attend the Project Management workshop next Tuesday, March 23. The session will run from 8:30 A.M. to 4:00 P.M. and will be held in the Mississippi Training Room. Please read the attached five-page document before coming to the class; it contains information you'll need for more advanced content material we'll be covering. Please feel free to contact me with any questions.

See you next Tuesday,

Ellen

Ellen Smilanich, Senior Training and Development Specialist

email@companyname.com, xxx-xxx-xxxx

Post-Classroom Sample

Greetings,

This is a reminder to practice the effective listening skills we covered in our class last week. When talking with others, ask yourself:

- What is he or she really saying?
- Am I hearing what he or she is saying or what I'm assuming is being said?
- Am I thinking about what to have for dinner tonight?

Feel free to contact me with any follow-up questions you may have.

Regards,

Diann

Diann Wilson, Senior Trainer

email@companyname.com, xxx-xxx-xxxx

13

Self-Study e-Learning

Cheyenne was responsible for the training for her company's new online self-service human resource program. Most of the employees were computer-savvy and locally situated, so she used traditional classroom training to introduce the concepts, benefits, and basic functionality, followed by e-learning solutions to provide ongoing support and training opportunities. Also, since many members of the company's sales force worked from their home offices and were unavailable for classroom training, she added a variation to meet their specific needs and provided their original instructor-led training session using online presentation software.

For the more advanced, content-specific material, Cheyenne used a combination of technology-based training (TBT) programs and knowledge databases. In the original classes, Cheyenne incorporated hands-on exercises using the "help" knowledge database of the software to teach the basic features and also to get her participants used to the idea that they would continue to have this assistance available to them long after they attended the classroom training session.

Since the vendor who built the software also provided TBT modules for the more advanced features, Cheyenne used these to provide ongoing training opportunities in two ways. First, she scheduled and advertised "open lab" sessions for people to use the TBTs in a computer training room away from their everyday job responsibilities. Her presence at the open labs was only required as a support person; most people had no trouble using the TBTs on their own, but she was available for troubleshooting if necessary and for answering questions that were not covered in the computerized programs. She also placed the TBTs on the company's intranet and followed each initial training session with a series of e-mails, directing participants to the TBTs and encouraging them to take advantage of their availability. For Cheyenne, using a variety of training solutions meant that the program accommodated different learning styles as well as the various working environments of the employees.

What Is Self-Study e-Learning?

Since e-learning is any training technique in which the primary delivery method is electronic and content is delivered via the Internet, intranet/extranet, audio or video technology, and/or CD-ROM, *self-study e-learning* (also known as asynchronous e-learning) is those electronic training solutions that are generally accessed by the learners without an instructor and on their own time. In this chapter, we'll discuss the self-study e-learning solutions of technology-based training and knowledge databases. We'll outline how to use each of these to enhance the content learned in a classroom as well as encourage the participants to transfer the learning into changes in their behavior back on the job.

Technology-Based Training Programs

Computer-based training (CBT), web-based training (WBT), alternative delivery, and online modules are all types of technology-based training programs (TBTs). While these terms aren't identical, they are similar enough to discuss their use and development in common terms. We refer to all of these as TBTs and define them as those training programs designed primarily for self-study use and usually delivered via CD-ROM or over the Internet/intranet.

Their quality varies widely in terms of interactivity, sophistication, and specificity. For example, many TBTs are little more than online books. They are designed so the learner reads a page of information, clicks a *Next* button, reads the following page, and so on. While these may even have simple multiple-choice "tests" built in, they generally do not deliver information in ways that are similar to how the participants will actually use the material and so may be boring and ineffective. They are often, however, relatively inexpensive to develop and/or purchase. At the other end of the spectrum are TBTs designed with a great deal of interactivity, offering the course content in interesting and even exciting ways and including company- and/or job-specific content. The best TBTs, as is true for any training, deliver content that is situation-specific in a manner that closely resembles how the participants will actually use the information back on the job.

TBTs can be purchased off-the-shelf or developed to meet specific learning objectives. Off-the-shelf programs are less expensive, of course, but often lack enough specificity to make them directly applicable to participants' jobs. On the other hand, developing a TBT program can run the gamut from being relatively inexpensive for simple programs to enormously expensive for complex ones, requiring the skills of programmers, instructional designers, graphic artists, audio specialists, and project managers.

Knowledge Databases

A knowledge database can be defined as an organized repository of useful information. Technically, knowledge databases are more electronic performance support solutions rather than training solutions; their primary purpose is to provide information when needed rather than teach new skills or knowledge. We include them here, however, since they have been widely used in recent years and because they are an excellent way to blend and support other training solutions by providing an easy and effective way for learners to use the information back at their jobs.

Common knowledge databases include the help files found within commercial software programs, online telephone books, lists of frequently asked questions, and even the Internet itself, in a broad manner of speaking. Generally, knowledge databases are used in technology departments, although this has changed somewhat as more and more employees become computer savvy. Some pros and cons of self-study e-learning are listed below.

Pros

- Can provide interesting and alternative learning methods;
- Leaves training resources more available for development work, since they aren't required for delivery;
- Allows for time flexibility and is delivered when the participants' time schedule allows; and
- Allows the participants to access the training in sections rather than all at once.

Cons

- Can be overlooked by busy employees;
- Requires a certain level of computer literacy;
- Requires specialized equipment; and
- Calls for employees to be self-motivated.

When to Use Self-Study e-Learning

Generally speaking, self-study e-learning solutions are more effective when the following conditions exist:

- The intended audience is very comfortable with technology;
- The content is relatively stable (especially in the case of TBTs);
- The intended users are motivated to learn the content; and
- The intended participants work a variety of time shifts.

The Intended Audience Is Very Comfortable with Technology. If the members of your intended audience are not comfortable with using computer technology, even the most well-designed self-study e-learning solutions may not be used adequately. You can still choose to implement them, but keep in mind that you may need to overcome resistance, provide education on e-learning benefits, and even supply training on the technology itself before your participants will encounter the content you're attempting to provide.

The Content Is Relatively Stable. Knowledge databases and TBTs are excellent choices when your content isn't going to change a great deal, since developing and maintaining e-learning solutions can be expensive. If your training content changes on an ongoing basis, other solutions may provide more return on your investment. This is especially true of technology-based training programs. The "page-turner" TBTs are relatively inexpensive to update (but are less effective in providing real learning). Sophisticated, highly interactive TBTs require a great deal of special expertise to reprogram, and many organizations simply allow them to become out-of-date when the content changes.

The Intended Users Are Motivated to Learn the Content. If your intended participants are motivated to learn the new content (because they're personally interested, their managers provide enough encouragement, or their jobs depend on it), they'll find the time to do so. But if they can succeed in their jobs without learning the new skills or knowledge, they may ignore any self-study programs, even if you're successful in alerting them to their existence. You can address this resistance by making sure you obtain active and visible management support and by involving key members of the intended audience in the design and development of the program.

The Intended Participants Work a Variety of Time Shifts. Self-study courses of any kind are helpful when delivering training to people working a variety of hours and shifts. Finding a time to schedule all of these people at one time, for example, can be difficult or even impossible, but with self-study e-learning, they can take the training at their own pace and when their schedule permits.

How to Implement Self-Study e-Learning

The implementation of self-study e-learning solutions varies greatly, as the complexity and sophistication of each program can vary greatly. Since we can't address the entire range of complexity and sophistication levels, we discuss common implementation steps below, generally including steps and examples from each extreme—from relatively simple and straightforward solutions to highly interactive and sophisticated ones.

Technology-Based Training Programs

To successfully use TBTs assumes that you have either purchased or developed well-designed ones; it is critical that they be sophisticated enough to meet or exceed the expectations of the participants, that they offer enough (and appropriate) interactivity, and that they be specific enough for the participants to recognize how they can use the information in their jobs. Use the steps below when designing and developing a TBT (we assume that you've already completed a needs analysis and determined that a TBT is one of the best solutions).

1. Determine the delivery method.
2. Select the appropriate people to develop the TBT.
3. Decide on the TBT's look and feel (formal? playful? incorporating standard company colors, fonts, and logos?).
4. Determine the type and sophistication of the interactivity.
5. Design and develop the TBT.
6. Develop and implement a communication plan.
7. Distribute the TBT.

1. Determine the Delivery Method. You have several choices on how to deliver the TBT programs. Many TBT programs today are delivered over an intranet or on the Internet, housed in an online "library" where employees can access programs as they need them or as they become aware of them. Another common delivery method is via CD-ROM. Yet another is via an "open lab," where participants can come to a computer training room to use the TBTs. The open lab approach has the benefits of allowing the participants to escape from the distractions of their day-to-day jobs and providing them with an onsite person who isn't delivering the training but who is available for questions, discussion, and technical support.

2. Select the Appropriate People to Develop the TBT. TBTs vary greatly in their level of sophistication. Simple ones (from a technical perspective) can be created relatively easily by nontechnical people using some of the more recent development software programs (some of which are listed in the Resources section at the end of this chapter). Many such programs allow computer-savvy instructional designers to design and develop TBT programs that can be delivered over the Internet/intranet or via CD-ROM.

However, if you are creating a highly interactive and sophisticated program, you may require the skills of a large variety of experts, including programmers, instructional designers, graphic artists, video technicians, audio specialists, and project managers, among others. The technical aspect of the design, development, delivery, and ongoing maintenance for this level of sophisticated program requires expertise in programming skills, even if you decide to use a software program that promises to provide pre-programmed design elements and interactivities. Technical expertise is invaluable in creating well-designed, defect-free, and sophisticated TBT programs.

No matter how complex or sophisticated a program you're designing, using the expertise of instructional designers is critical. Unfortunately, as with many training programs, the up-front instructional design phase is often cut short or not done at all. This appears to be even more prevalent with TBT development. This problem can be easily addressed if the project manager and/or business leaders make it clear that instructional design is as important in the program's planning as are the technical aspects. Graphic artists can add polished and effective graphic design, which is demanded by many of today's computer-savvy employees. Video technicians and audio specialists are necessary if your TBT contains video and audio elements, and finally, project management is absolutely essential in planning and tracking all of the resources, budget, and timelines involved in a complex and highly technical TBT project.

3. **Decide on the TBT's Look and Feel.** This step is critical to the success of the TBT program, and it's well worth the time and effort required to discover what look and feel will appeal to the intended users. The choice of font styles and colors is somewhat subjective, but a great deal of research has been conducted that indicates certain fonts and colors tend to be more effective when viewed on a screen rather than on a printed page. You also must determine the "feel" of the program by researching the interests and expectations of those who will use the training. Engineers, for example, may sneer at any cartoon characters,

while teachers may be very open to them. Experienced and computer-savvy users will demand a more sophisticated look and feel, while you can get away with a more basic approach for those who are relatively new to computer use.

4. Determine the Type and Sophistication of the Interactivity. This step is closely related to the previous one, and the same limitations and expectations exist on the part of the intended audience. The more expert the computer user, the more demanding he or she will be in terms of expecting sophisticated, highly interactive programming and a professional look and feel. Remember that all interactivity should be designed with an eye to the specific learning objectives. Some TBT designers will use a program's built-in interactivity features because they are impressive, without considering whether the interactivity successfully teaches any content that has been identified as critical to the learning purpose of the program. As with all instructional design, the most successful interactions are those that mimic the environment where the participant will use the new skills or knowledge, appear to be directly applicable to the user's work life, and provide content and interactivity that are interesting to the intended participants.

5. Design and Develop the TBT. If your TBT is relatively straightforward, designing and developing it may be as simple as entering your content into presentation software or into a "wizard" provided by some of the development software programs available today. If your TBT requires a more extensive group of developers, they will create the TBT using one of the typical development approaches, such as waterfall or rapid application design (RAD). The waterfall method is a linear process of gathering requirements, designing, developing, testing, and moving into production. RAD, on the other hand, is a much more circular development cycle, in which each core element is designed and reviewed, developed and reviewed, and where testing occurs as each element is completed rather than at the end of the lifecycle. The actual development of TBTs is a complex process that is significantly different from standard training solutions and beyond the scope of this book. Many excellent resources exist, however, and we encourage you to use them either to teach you the specifics of TBT development and/or for assistance in hiring the right people to complete the development for you. We include a list of these resources at the end of the chapter in the Resources section.

6. Develop and Implement a Communication Plan. TBT programs are most effective when they are readily available, visible to the intended users, and easy to access. A communication plan is essential for announcing their availability, intended audience, and benefits to the participants and to the organization. The plan should also communicate how and when users can access the new training opportunity. Consider offering a demonstration of the TBT to help overcome any resistance to using technology-driven learning solutions.

7. Distribute the TBT. The distribution of the TBT will vary depending on the delivery method selected at the beginning of the development cycle. If you've chosen to deliver it over your intranet, for example, the distribution can be as simple as moving it to the designated website and announcing its availability by including a link to the site in your e-mail announcement. Distribution via CD-ROM requires the actual production of the CDs as well as the physical delivery of the CDs to the employees who will use them. Using an "open lab" to deliver the TBT may be a good idea, particularly if you expect any resistance from your employees. An open lab will require loading and testing the TBTs on the training room workstations (or loading and testing the URLs, if delivering via the intranet), scheduling and communicating the availability of the open lab sessions, and conducting the labs themselves, all of which will be a good investment of time if it helps your employees become more comfortable using this new and effective training solution.

Knowledge Databases

The effectiveness of a knowledge database depends largely on how well its organization and lingo serve the expectations of those who are intended to use it. Knowledge databases are often designed and built by computer programmers who assume that the intended users have the same expertise, terminology, and expectations they do. This is a natural assumption, but one that can result in a knowledge database that is ignored instead of used, once the participants learn that the information provided isn't helpful to them. For this reason, we highly recommend that the structure and terminology, in particular, be developed and tested by a representative group of the intended users. You can use the following steps when designing and developing a knowledge database:

1. Gather detailed requirements.

2. Design the database.

3. Develop the database.

4. Test the database.

5. Create a communication plan.

6. Move the database into production.

7. Promote use of the database.

1. Gather Detailed Requirements. Requirements are used in software development and are basically the same as learning objectives: They describe something that the program must be able to do or a quality that the program must have. As in any training program design, the more time and effort spent on up-front analysis—gathering and documenting detailed requirements—the more likely you will be to meet the needs of the intended users. In building knowledge databases, these requirements might include:

- Amount and detail of the information needed, including terminology used to either ask questions or provide the answers to the questions posed by the end-users;

- An organizational structure that is logical from the users' perspectives (which may or may not be the same as the programmers' perspectives);

- How the database will be accessed (from a website, embedded within a software program, on a CD-ROM);

- The graphical user interface (GUI)—what learners see when they access the database;

- Performance expectations (How fast will screens and data refresh? How many people will be accessing the database at the same time?); and/or

- Reporting capabilities, if any.

2. **Design the Database.** When detailed and unambiguous requirements are gathered, designing the knowledge database is relatively easy. You have to determine which software will be used to build the database, the organizational structure of the content, the delivery method, the look and feel of the screens, and whether any reporting capabilities are needed or desired. Ideally, all of these decisions will be made and tested before moving on to the development phase, although, in actual practice, development often begins as soon as the preliminary decisions are made.

How organized and how useful the database is depends largely on how well its design reflects the needs and characteristics of its intended audience. For example, "help files" written into commercial software can be described as knowledge databases, and as software users know, some are written in such cryptic terms that they are almost useless when you're trying to find out how to perform a specific task within the software. The most effective knowledge databases are built using the terminology, organizational structure, and computer literacy levels of the intended users.

3. **Develop the Database.** The development phase of the knowledge database involves the actual building of the database structure, the writing and editing of the knowledge content, the construction of the GUI, and the creation of the delivery system.

4. **Test the Database.** Testing is most effective when done throughout the development process and on different levels. First, each component of the database has to be tested individually (unit test); then each has to be tested to see how well it works with the other components (integration test). Finally, the entire database has to be tested (system test/user test). Generally the unit, integration, and system testing is done by programmers/developers, and the user test is completed by members of the intended audience.

5. **Create a Communication Plan**. As with TBT, knowledge databases are most effective when they are readily available, visible to the intended users, and easy to access. Develop a communication plan to announce the availability of the new training support programs, their intended audience, and the benefits to the participants and the organization.

6. **Move the Database into Production**. Once testing is complete, you can move the database into production. If the testing was thorough and any defects were resolved, this step can often be accomplished with little to no effort, compared with the previous phases. Keep in mind, however, that, once the database is in production, your responsibilities don't end. In order to continue to meet the needs of the end-users, the content will have to be reviewed and updated and the performance will have to be monitored and any problems addressed. We recommend that you create a schedule of semi-annual or annual reviews and assign a specific workgroup or individual the responsibility of making sure these steps are completed. We also recommend that the responsibility of ongoing technical maintenance of the database be assigned and documented early in the development process—the earlier the better.

7. **Promote Use of the Database**. Because of the unique motivational needs (addressed at the beginning of this section), your knowledge databases will be most successful if you actively advertise and promote their use. You can do this by offering training on how to use them and including real-life hands-on activities. You can also advertise them by sending e-mails with updated information. Another method is to sponsor contests such as scavenger hunts and offer prizes to the employees who find all of the information. Provide ongoing reminders to help the intended users begin to rely on the new source of information as they perform their day-to-day activities. The critical component in all of this is to make sure that the knowledge database contains information that your intended users need and desire, that they know it does, and that they are familiar enough with how to access it that using it becomes almost second-nature.

How to Blend Self-Study e-Learning with Classroom Training

TBTs and knowledge databases can both be successfully blended with classroom training, although in different ways.

Technology-Based Training Programs

A TBT can be used in a variety of ways before, during, or after a classroom training session. For example, you could require participants to successfully complete a TBT program containing basic information before coming to the classroom session, where you can concentrate on testing their knowledge of the basics and moving on to the more advanced content areas. This approach will be most successful if the participants are motivated to complete prerequisites, either because they're used to doing so and are particularly interested in the content or because your training program has strong, visible, and active support of the participants' senior management.

Using TBTs during a classroom session can provide interest and add an alternative method to traditional classroom techniques. Because TBTs are self-study, most of the participants will be occupied while working through them, allowing you time to focus on learners who may be less knowledgeable about the content and who may need extra personal attention. Depending on the design of the TBT, you can use them to introduce new material or to provide a review and/or practice of material that you've previously covered. Training programs for standard software are particularly conducive to including TBTs in the classroom session; they're relatively inexpensive, for one thing, and can be useful in teaching basic features of the software that you can then supplement with more situation- and job-specific examples and content.

TBTs can also be used after classroom sessions, for review and practice purposes. We've found it to be especially successful if we provide reminders for the participants, either by sending e-mails or by scheduling an open lab where they can get away from their day-to-day responsibilities.

Knowledge Databases

Knowledge databases can also be blended with classroom training in a variety of ways. Within the classroom session, for example, you might build in exercises requiring the participants to use the database in order to successfully complete tasks. This type of exercise is particularly helpful if you intend for them to use the knowledge database on an ongoing basis in their day-to-day job responsibilities. You'll be most successful if you create exercises with real-life scenarios that require them to use the database in the same manner in which they'll use it on the job.

You might also follow the classroom training session with a series of activities requiring them to use the database, either distributing the activities at the end of the session or sending them via e-mail at pre-announced time intervals. As with TBTs, you may wish to schedule an open lab where the participants can complete the activities without the distractions of their telephones, e-mail, and co-workers.

Examples of successful blending with classroom training include:

- An electronic scavenger hunt for new employees, intended to familiarize them with the company's internal and external websites. This approach could be used either before or after the classroom training session.

- Using technology-based training to learn how to insert graphics into a document after learning basic word processing in the classroom.

- An open lab of technology-based training to be held after classroom training for company practices, intended to reinforce basic information introduced in the classroom session.

KEY POINTS

- Self-study e-learning solutions are different from other training methods in that they are generally accessed by the learners without an instructor and on their own time.

- These solutions include knowledge databases and technology-based training programs.

- Self-motivation is critical with these types of solutions because your learners will have to choose to use the programs without the benefit of having a trainer there to encourage and support them.

- The development and the maintenance of these solutions require technical expertise.

RESOURCES

Driscoll, M. (2002). *Web-based training: Designing e-learning experiences* (with CD-ROM). San Francisco, CA: Pfeiffer. Describes how to design web-based training programs and includes charts, tables, and checklists.

Hernandez, M. J. (2003). *Database design for mere mortals: A hands-on guide to relational database design* (2nd ed.). Reading, MA: Addison-Wesley. A common-sense approach to designing relational databases.

Horton, W. (2000). *Designing web-based training*. Hoboken, NJ: John Wiley & Sons. Describes what web-based training is, its advantages and disadvantages, and how to design, build, and evaluate a WBT program. Designed for non-technical people, it also includes discussion on how to implement WBT using learning theories.

Horton, W., & Horton, K. (2003). *e-Learning tools and technologies: A consumer's guide for trainers, teachers, educators, and instructional designers*. Hoboken, NJ: John Wiley & Sons. A consumer's guide for trainers, teachers, educators, and instructional designers to identify, evaluate, and choose products and services based on different e-learning scenarios.

Robertson, S., & Robertson, J. (1999). *Mastering the requirements process*. Reading, MA: Addison-Wesley. Includes the steps, methodologies, and examples needed to gather, document, and use requirements software development. While it was written for software engineers, a computer-savvy instructional designer will still benefit from the information, especially since requirements gathering in software development so closely resembles the determining goals and learning objectives step in the instructional design process.

WEBSITES

This listing contains websites that describe software that may assist you in designing and delivering self-study e-learning solutions. It is not an endorsement of any of the tools and services, but is intended simply as an aid for you in beginning your search.

www.blackboard.com
www.desire2learn.com
www.embanet.com
www.microsoft.com/windows/netmeeting.com
www.WebCT.com
www.webex.com

14

Job Aids

Steve was looking forward to his new job as a service representative for a city planning office. During his first three weeks of work, he learned his new job responsibilities by participating in classroom training, where he was introduced to all of the services that the city planning department provides to developers and builders. The training consisted of a combination of lecture and practice. Steve first practiced with the instructor playing the role of a customer and then advanced to handling actual customer calls while the instructor listened in and assisted.

After the training period was over, Steve was assigned to a desk in the planning office and had customer calls routed to him regularly. He was by himself (no instructor), but not alone. The city had developed a comprehensive reference guide for all of the service representatives. The guide was introduced to Steve in the classroom and was easily accessible, positioned on his desk between the phone and the computer screen. Tabs indicated the major categories (codes, forms, scheduling, and so forth), and laminated pages kept the much-used job aid in good condition.

As some of the simpler or more routine requests came in, Steve was able to remember what he had just learned in the classroom, so he could easily answer those questions and provide information. However, when more complicated requests were received or questions were asked about codes or exceptions to policies, Steve found himself referring to his reference guide.

The guide was kept in a three-ring binder, allowing for easy revisions or additions as the city grew and codes changed. The combination of classroom training and the reference guide served as a perfect mix of training solutions for Steve's needs. Even after two years on the job, the guide still provided him with the support and answers he needed to be effective in his job.

What Is a Job Aid?

A job aid is a tool or resource containing information, processes, or perspectives designed to support work and activity and direct or guide performance. Effective job aids provide useful data, answering questions about who, what, how, when, or where, and are organized by the user's frame of reference. Instead of being expected to remember information, employees can rely on job aids to complete a task that might be infrequent or new. Job aids can be tools used to perform a specific task, step-by-step instructions on when and how to perform tasks, or a systematic approach to the most common practices or techniques. They can also save time in troubleshooting, because they can provide clear and concise information. All of us use job aids in our everyday lives. Examples include:

- It's time to file your taxes, but you don't find the IRS forms to be self-explanatory, so you turn to the instruction manual you picked up with your forms.

- You want to organize your computer files, but you can't figure out how to create a folder, so you turn to the online help provided within the program.

- You want to record a television program using your VCR, so you refer to the VCR manual.

- You have a leaking faucet that you don't know how to repair. Since you don't know a plumber, you turn to the phone book, which provides you with the information needed to locate a plumber.

Job aids can take a variety of forms. Some of the more common are:

- Step-by-step instructions;
- Worksheets or forms;
- Decision tables;
- Flowcharts;
- Checklists;
- Reference manuals;
- Electronic performance support systems (EPSS);
- Procedure guides;
- Troubleshooting guides; and
- Performance coaching tools.

Step-by-Step Instructions. Step-by-step instructions are most often used for building or assembling products. They contain directions on what to do, how to do it, and in what order. They are often accompanied by photos or drawings to help demonstrate how a job is to be done. In a manufacturing environment, step-by-step instructions allow employees to assemble each product in the exact same order and in the exact same way. These job aids can be in a hard-copy, printed format or may be available online. Step-by-step instructions ensure consistency and can enhance the quality of any task or product. We've included a sample step-by-step instruction sheet in Exhibit 14.1 at the end of the chapter.

Worksheets or Forms. These are fill-in-the-blank templates that are designed to lead employees to consider and complete specific information to help accomplish a task or procedure. They may be used as standalone training solutions or they may be used to reinforce what was learned in a classroom training setting. For example, a worksheet can be given to managers to help them prepare to give effective feedback to one of their employees—reinforcing effective feedback skills that were taught in a class. A sample worksheet is provided at the end of this chapter in Exhibit 14.2.

Decision Tables. Decision tables lay out (in tabular form) all possible situations that a decision may encompass and specify which action to take in each of these. You can use decision tables in your projects to clarify complex decision-making situations. They are commonly used in the computer field and provide employees with a consistent methodology for making a variety of work decisions. We include a sample decision table in Exhibit 14.3 at the end of the chapter.

Flowcharts. A flowchart is a pictorial representation showing all of the steps of a process. A flowchart is used for:

- Defining and analyzing processes;
- Building a step-by-step picture of a process; and/or
- Standardizing or finding areas for improvement in a process.

Flowcharts are frequently used in engineering, information technology, and manufacturing work environments.

Checklists. A checklist is an inventory of factors, properties, aspects, components, criteria, tasks, or dimensions needed to be completed or considered in order to perform a certain job. A variety of types of checklists exist; they range from a simple list to those containing numerous, sequential items that must be completed in order. Checklists also ensure consistency. For example, the pre-flight checklist ensures safe flying for those who travel by air. See the end of this chapter for an example in Exhibit 14.4.

Reference Manuals. While a reference manual may contain many of the other listed job aids, it is usually a more comprehensive guidebook, typically covering many aspects of many tasks. In Steve's situation, his manual provided information on the city's policies, codes, and procedures. Reference manuals are useful for employees who must have information on a variety of products or a great deal of detailed or technical information. Usually written by technical writers, these job aids are most effective when organized by the *user's* frame of reference.

Electronic Performance Support Systems (EPSS). An electronic performance support system is an online resource that is available to and easily accessible by employees. It is structured to provide immediate, individualized online access to a full range of information and tools. An EPSS can also be described as any computer program that improves employee performance by reducing the complexity or number of steps required to perform a task, providing the information an employee needs to perform a task, or providing a decision support system that enables an employee to identify the action that is appropriate for a particular set of conditions.

An EPSS can take the form of a job aid or may be used to manage information within an organization. (See Chapter 13, "Self-Study e-Learning.") When used as a job aid, an EPSS can help an organization reduce the cost of training staff while increasing productivity and performance by providing information online as a follow-up to a training class.

Procedure Guides. Procedure guides respond directly to the need for employees to follow rules and guidelines for specific jobs. They may cover one task or a multitude of practical and pertinent tasks in areas such as programming and troubleshooting. To be effective, a procedure guide should offer a simple layout with easy-to-follow, step-by-step instructions designed to help employees become highly effective and proficient. We include a sample table of contents for a procedure guide at the end of this chapter in Exhibit 14.5.

Troubleshooting Guides. In any organization, downtime means lower productivity, which in turn means less profit. Troubleshooting guides eliminate the time that is often wasted while employees search through cumbersome technical manuals looking for the solution to a problem. The most effective troubleshooting guides are product-specific, focused on best practices, and contain easy-to-use flowcharts and graphics. Troubleshooting guides are valuable "just-in-time" resources that offer immediate assistance for most troubleshooting situations.

Performance Coaching Tools. These job aids serve to support knowledge by providing suggestions, tips, motivation, or advice (rather than directions) on using a skill. Performance coaching job aids support questions such as "Why is this important?" and "What might I consider before I make this decision?" Frequently, performance coaching job aids support performance in new, difficult, or ambiguous tasks such as supervisory approaches for motivating employees. The term "coaching"—when used in this context—is different from coaching as a training solution (as discussed in Chapter 16).

Some pros and cons of using job aids are listed below.

Pros

- Help employees transfer skills from the training session to the job site;
- Can help reduce the length of training;
- Provide workers with instant access to the information they need;
- Efficiently supplement training;
- Can save resources by enabling less training, or possibly even no training; and
- Provide a practical training resource that employees will use.

Cons

- Can increase levels of frustration if poorly written;
- May become out-of-date;
- More complex ones may be costly or time-consuming to produce;
- May require specialized skills to develop;
- Require resources to keep them current; and
- May not be used if the selected medium is not convenient to use.

When to Use Job Aids

There are many situations in which a job aid is useful. Consider using a job aid when:

- A new task is to be performed;

- A task will be performed infrequently;

- The situation is complex;

- There are significant consequences for error;

- Employees must access a large amount or changing bodies of knowledge;

- Resources are not sufficient to support classroom training; and/or

- You want to enhance classroom training and increase the likelihood of actual behavioral change back on the job.

As with any training solution, job aids are not perfect for every situation. Job aids would not be appropriate or effective when employees are not motivated or are unaccustomed to consulting references, situations are novel or unpredictable, or users lack the reading or visual skills to use a job aid.

How to Implement Job Aids

Job aids can be one of the easiest training solutions to implement. The number of people who need the training, the content to be learned, and the availability of appropriate resources to develop the job aid all influence the decision to use job aids. The steps of job aid implementation follow:

1. Choose the format and the medium.

2. Prepare the job aid draft.

3. Pilot the job aid.

4. Make revisions.

5. Manage the job aid.

1. Choose the Format and the Medium

The amount and type of content, as well as the reading level and computer literacy of the learners, will help you determine which type of job aid to select and how to format the type you choose. As we mentioned earlier, an effective job aid is designed from the user's frame of reference. For example, in Steve's situation, the reference guide was organized using tabs to indicate major headings such as policies and forms. This is the order in which Steve would need to use the guide, and the design helped him use the tool quickly and efficiently.

2. Prepare the Job Aid Draft

Once the type of job aid has been selected, the aid has to be drafted. Larger, more complex job aids may have to be drafted by a technical writer. A SME or a trainer can create simpler, shorter aids. In preparing the job aid draft, include pertinent general information, answer the questions "how" and "when," emphasize actions by highlighting verbs, and present actions as steps in the order in which they must be followed. Be sure to use white space and graphics when appropriate to add interest and readability.

3. Pilot the Job Aid

Before making copies and introducing a job aid to a large audience, pilot or test the job aid on a smaller population. Piloting allows you to discover which elements of the job aid are useful and which, if any, are ineffective. The completeness and accuracy of the content can be evaluated, and you will learn whether the content is in a logical order from the users' perspectives.

4. Make Revisions

Based on feedback from the participants in the pilot group, make improvements to the job aid before copying and distributing it to large audiences.

5. Manage the Job Aid

Assign ownership to each job aid to ensure that it is kept current. As procedures change or new products are introduced, the information contained in a job aid will have to be modified as well. Online job aids may require both content and technical owners, as the person with the knowledge of the content may not have the technical skills to modify computer software or files.

Owners should regularly monitor their job aids, and a system should be devised to ensure that any out-of-date hard-copy job aids are discarded or replaced by more current copies. The frequency of the reviews is determined by the stability of the content contained in the job aids. The reviews can be scheduled as frequently as once a month or as infrequently as once a year.

How to Blend Job Aids with Classroom Training

To successfully blend job aids with classroom training, ensure that they have a look similar to the classroom materials and follow in the same order. While different instructional designers may be designing the classroom training and the job aids, the elements must be coordinated to create an interconnected learning experience. Job aids and class materials (handouts, slides, and so forth) do not have to look identical, but they should be formatted for a similar appearance and feel. Using consistent graphic elements and learning strategies will create a familiar feeling for users. This helps participants to connect what was learned in the classroom with the job aid they will use on the job. Something as simple as the consistent use of fonts, colors, and layouts may help the learner recognize the content and more effectively move from learning to actual behavioral change. If examples or scenarios are used in both the classroom and job aids, use the same or similar scenarios.

A logical rollout schedule depends on the complexity of the skill or volume of information being learned. With more complex or lengthy job aids, it is important for users to learn how the job aid is organized and to practice with it so they can efficiently use it on the job. In these situations, we recommend using the job aid throughout the classroom experience. For example, in Steve's situation, he was learning a large volume of information, and his job aid—the reference guide—supported the information taught in the classroom. Therefore, the logical sequence was to introduce and use the job aid in the classroom training. Job aids that are online are also frequently introduced in the classroom, where participants can practice accessing the tool while an instructor is present to provide any needed assistance or to answer questions.

Other shorter or simpler job aids may be implemented before, after, or apart from classroom training. For example, distributing a job aid outlining a new file maintenance procedure before the class would allow employees to read about the procedure and even practice it prior to attending class. Participants would then be able to ask questions of the instructor based on their experience with the job aid.

As another example, when introducing a new process for ordering supplies, you may want to explain what the process is and why it was changed before providing employees with step-by-step instructions. In this situation, the job aid might be implemented after the classroom training. And in cases of very basic information, such as a checklist of standard items included in a mailing, the job aids could be provided without any classroom training at all. In addition, some well-constructed electronic performance support systems are intuitive enough that computer-savvy employees can rely on them with no classroom training required.

Typically, adding job aids to your other learning solutions requires no special executive approval or involvement. It simply requires you to determine where it would be helpful to have a resource, create that resource, and then make it available.

Examples of successful blending of job aids with classroom training include:

- Classroom safety training that includes the distribution of material safety data sheets for use back on the job.

- A checklist for new employees that is distributed prior to a classroom orientation program.

- A classroom training session on giving effective feedback, followed a week later with a performance coaching tool to remind and encourage participants to use the skills taught in the classroom.

See Chapters 5 through 7 for additional information on how to blend training solutions.

KEY POINTS

- Decide which form of job aid is most appropriate for the subject matter being covered (step-by-step instructions, flowchart, and so forth).

- Design all job aids with the end user in mind. Put information in a logical order for the person who will use the job aid.

- Introducing job aids in a class will increase the likelihood that they will be used back on the job.

RESOURCES

Frank, D. (1996). *Terrific training materials: High-impact graphic designs for workbooks, handouts, instructor guides, and job aids.* Amherst, MA: HRD Press. Introduces graphic design principles and demonstrates how to use them to make printed training materials more effective.

Rossett, A., & Gautier-Downes, J. (1991). *A handbook of job aids.* San Francisco, CA: Pfeiffer. How to create and implement a variety of types of job aids so employees can easily find information.

Stimson, N. (2002). *How to write and prepare training materials.* London, UK: Kogan Page. A handbook of essential techniques to use when writing and preparing all types of training materials, whether handouts or online job aids.

Exhibit 14.1. Sample Step-by Step Instructions.

Instructions for Completing an Online Purchase

1. Select the item that you wish to purchase by double clicking on the item name in the **Purchase Now** screen.

2. Enter your name, mailing and shipping address, phone number, and e-mail address in the spaces provided.

3. Enter your credit card and billing information in the boxes.

4. Click on the **Confirm Order** button at the bottom of the page.

5. A copy of the items you have ordered will appear, along with billing and shipping information. If you see any errors in this information, click the red **Go Back** button at the bottom left side of the screen and correct the information before proceeding. If the information is correct, click the green **Order Now** button at the bottom right side of the screen.

6. Your order confirmation will appear on the screen. Print a copy of this for your files.

7. A confirmation will be sent to you within twenty-four hours containing a link to a website where you can check on the status of your order.

Exhibit 14.2. Sample Worksheet.

This worksheet can be used following a class on Giving Effective Feedback to help participants prepare for giving feedback to their employees.

Name of feedback recipient: _____

Desired outcome of the feedback:

Describe what he or she did that you would like to see changed:

What was the impact of his or her behavior?

How would you prefer he or she behave?

How can you express confidence in his or her ability to change the behavior?

When do you plan to give this feedback?

Exhibit 14.3. Sample Decision Table.

An employee of a construction company needs to make a decision regarding building some new rental units near a college. The construction choices are (1) to build a four-unit apartment complex; (2) to build an eight-unit complex; or (3) do nothing. The college may grow, hold steady, or shrink in size, but no one is able to place any probabilities on these scenarios. In consultation with the finance department, the decision table below was developed to show the conditional payoffs.

	Shrink	Steady	Grow
Build Four	−$20,000	$70,000	$80,000
Build Eight	−$60,000	$100,000	$170,000
Do Nothing	$0	$0	$0

Exhibit 14.4. Sample Checklist.

Instructions: Use the following checklist to decide whether or not to place an employee on a corrective action plan (CAP).

Yes	No	Item
☐	☐	Have you given the employee verbal feedback on his or her performance?
☐	☐	Did you give the employee written feedback on his or her performance?
☐	☐	Have you offered assistance (training, mentoring) to improve the performance?
☐	☐	Did you describe the preferred performance?
☐	☐	Have you completed and signed a CAP form?
☐	☐	Have you verbally communicated the information on the form to the employee?
☐	☐	Did you present the signed form to the employee?
☐	☐	Have you placed a copy of the signed form in the employee's personnel file?

Exhibit 14.5. Sample Table of Contents for a Procedure Guide.

15

Mentoring

Molly was hired as a program manager in a manufacturing company, right out of college. She was armed with lots of theoretical knowledge but little practical experience. One of her responsibilities was to lead a cross-functional team designed to ensure that new products were quickly and effortlessly introduced in the manufacturing plant where she worked. While Molly had ample education in both new product design and introduction, she had no experience in leading a team. She quickly experienced a great deal of difficulty working with individuals with different priorities and in exerting influence with people whom she has no authority over.

Molly went to her boss, who recommended that she enroll in the company's project management course. This was an intensive, three-day class that covered all of the elements of project management, including project planning, scheduling, use of resources, evaluation, and even information on how to work with a team. The course was offered on-site, was only going to take three days of Molly's time, and contained the content Molly needed to successfully lead her project team.

Molly attended the course, learned a great deal, and was on the job Thursday morning, ready with information and knowledge to effectively lead her team. That afternoon, she held a team meeting. She applied what she had learned in class and established team ground rules, clearly stated the team's purpose, distributed a Gantt chart with key deadline dates, and discussed team member roles and responsibilities. She encouraged team participation and was pleased with the response from the team members. Clearly, the class had fully prepared her to be a more effective project manager.

However, the following Monday she received a frantic call from a harried plant manager. The new product Molly was assigned to manage suddenly had an accelerated schedule. The team needed to move the schedule forward by one month. Molly immediately got on the phone to tell the members of the cross-functional team that they would have to commit to doing everything much more quickly. She was shocked with the responses she received. People had other priorities. One team member had a two-week vacation planned and wasn't willing to reschedule. Without the help of her teammates, she would not be able to meet the new project schedule. She grabbed the workbook from her class and frantically flipped through the pages looking for the section on last-minute schedule changes. There was none. Her boss was out of the office, and she wasn't sure where to turn. Then she remembered the mentoring program that was discussed in the project management class.

Molly called her classroom instructor and explained her dilemma. Fortunately, the company's formal mentoring program was scheduled to start soon. Molly was able to enroll right away and was paired with Jeri, a senior project manager from a different department who had been with the company for seven years. Jeri had worked with several different cross-functional project teams and had successfully managed them through numerous challenges.

Following a program orientation, Molly and Jeri met regularly once a week for an hour at a time. Jeri gave Molly sound advice on how to handle the schedule changes, including how to negotiate deadline dates with the plant manager. Jeri explained how she had worked with her team members in the past when similar situations occurred and was able to help Molly learn how to work with individuals in the organization to reach agreement on new schedules.

Molly was not only relieved, but she felt even better prepared to do her job. She was able to take the skills she learned in the classroom, combine them with the practical strategies that Jeri taught her, and apply them immediately to her own situation. Using this new, practical knowledge, Molly worked with the plant manager to renegotiate the project due date and was able to effectively pull her team together to meet the deadline. When the formal mentoring program was over, Jeri and Molly agreed to continue their relationship. The two maintained contact over the next three years, which helped Molly to enhance her career and her ability to achieve her goals as a program manager.

What Is Mentoring?

Mentoring is a partnership between two people that allows an individual with more experience (the mentor) to share skills, knowledge, and experience with an individual with less experience (the mentee or protégé). A mentor can be a counselor or guide, a tutor, or a teacher. Mentoring provides opportunities for individuals to grow and learn in an individual, supportive, and friendly environment. Mentoring can be an effective tool to transfer knowledge from one individual to another. It provides employees with something no other learning opportunity does—their own personalized teachers and champions.

Mentoring can be done in an informal manner or it can be managed as a formal program, like Molly and Jeri's situation, with multiple pairs of mentors and protégés working together. In most situations, a formal program has a better chance of success because it has defined objectives and a built-in evaluation. Some of the types of programs include:

- *Supervisory mentoring*—a normal function of the manager's duties. The effectiveness of this type of mentoring relates directly to the job as well as to the ability of the supervisor to pass on knowledge. Mentoring by supervisors typically takes the form of instruction—how to do a particular job or improve a skill.

- *Informal mentoring*—the unofficial pairing of two individuals. The pairs are drawn together and engage in a mentoring relationship built on common interests, chemistry, and trust. It is a natural pairing that occurs when a protégé finds a "kindred spirit" or a trusted advisor and teacher who helps him or her meet some personal or professional needs. Sometimes the mentor is not even aware of the role he or she is playing in this type of relationship.

- *New hire mentoring*—helps new employees to understand the organization's culture, products, and services and what it takes to be successful in the organization. Mentors typically help protégés understand how to navigate the company and how to build networks quickly. This type of relationship is usually a shorter-term one that lasts only throughout the assimilation of the employee into the organization.

- *Formal mentoring*—involves a commitment from the entire organization, as well as from the mentors, protégés, and their managers. A well-designed formal mentoring process pairs mentors and protégés, trains them to be successful, tracks success, and develops and implements a plan for helping the protégés learn key skills and competencies necessary for attaining career goals.

The potential advantages of participating in a mentoring relationship are great for the individuals being mentored, as well as for those doing the mentoring. However, mentoring is not necessarily a problem-free activity. Some pros and cons are listed below.

Pros

- Protégés gain increased skills and knowledge from other employees who are more experienced in the field;

- Protégés can develop professional self-confidence;

- Mentors can help protégés with the practical application of knowledge;

- Mentors can also be an important source of support to learners who are working to apply new skills;

- Individualized learning needs can be met;

- Mentors can be re-energized, as mentoring can provide them with a sense of importance and renewed enthusiasm for their roles; and

- Mentoring allows participants to work within their own schedules.

Cons

- Not all pairings work effectively;

- Formal mentoring programs require organizational resources to develop and maintain them;

- An adequate time commitment is required in order for the relationships to be successful;

- Pairs must take initiative to schedule time together; and

- Over-dependence can be a problem from either side of the relationship.

When to Use Mentoring

Mentoring can be useful in an organization with any of the following:

- Bimodal distribution of service in the workforce—a lot of newer employees and an equal number of experienced employees;

- Lack of leadership bench strength (employees available and qualified to move into leadership roles), or an under-representation of women or minorities in leadership ranks;

- Organizational need to transfer skills from one individual or group to another; and/or

- Desire to replicate success of key high performers.

How to Implement Mentoring

The steps listed below provide a high-level step-by-step overview of what to do to implement mentoring in an organization. Much of this information can be translated into a project plan, once you have the agreement to proceed from senior management.

Phase I: Prepare

1. Determine the need and purpose for mentoring.

2. Obtain management support for the program.

3. Identify a mentoring coordinator.

4. Make implementation decisions regarding:

    a. Time allotment

    b. Orientation/training strategy

    c. Communications strategy (to whom and how often?)

Phase II: Implement

5. Communicate the mentoring program to the organization.

6. Invite or appoint mentors and protégés.

7. Pair mentors with protégés.

8. Orient/train mentors and protégés.

9. Develop the mentoring relationship.

10. Track progress.

Phase III: Evaluate

11. Distribute surveys to participants and analyze results.

12. Determine whether the program will continue.

Phase I: Prepare

1. **Determine the Need and Purpose for Mentoring.** The first step is to determine whether mentoring will be useful in your organization. There are various cir-

cumstances under which mentoring would be an effective training solution. Refer to the When to Use Mentoring section of this chapter to determine whether mentoring is appropriate for your situation.

2. **Obtain Management Support for the Program.** A mentoring program will require a time commitment outside of the employee's regular job, typically at least one hour a week. Because of this, it's important to ensure you have management support for the program before beginning implementation.

Much evidence exists in the literature about the benefits that a mentoring program can bring to an organization. An explanation of the program structure, purpose, time requirements, and expected results will typically convince senior management to support the program. We include a sample executive summary as Exhibit 15.1 at the end of this chapter.

3. **Identify a Mentoring Coordinator.** A coordinator is not needed for informal mentoring relationships, but is very important for formal programs. The training or human resources department most often coordinates the mentoring program within an organization. However, many successful programs have been run by a team of employees or by a line manager from operations. The coordinator has the responsibility for establishing program parameters, selecting and pairing participants, and managing implementation of the program.

4. **Make Implementation Decisions.** Decisions must be made on the following factors:

- *Time allotment*—Mentoring programs typically run from six months to one year. The length of the program is dependent on the volume of knowledge or skills that need to be passed on to the protégé.

- *Orientation/training strategy*—Every formal mentoring program requires some type of orientation or training to teach participants about their roles in the program, discuss time commitments, and review program guidelines and expectations. In addition to developing content, you also must decide whether the delivery will be done in person or through e-learning methodologies.

- *Communications strategy*—Finally, you will have to develop a communications strategy. The managers of the mentors and protégés also will have to be kept informed of the program, the time commitments, and their roles.

Phase II: Implement

5. Communicate the Mentoring Program to the Organization. Follow the strategy you outlined above and communicate with the mentors, protégés, and their managers. In addition, use existing communication channels to advise the entire organization of the program's existence. Employees will want to know how participants were selected, the purpose of the program, and how they can participate in any future mentoring programs. See the sample communication in Exhibit 15.2 at the end of this chapter.

6. Invite or Appoint Mentors and Protégés. Determine who should learn (protégé pool), what has to be learned, and who is available with the practical knowledge and skills that must be taught. Then decide whether you will allow people to self-select for the program or if you will take manager nominations or appointments. When selecting protégés, you may want to allow employees to apply for participation in the program if you have large numbers of people who have training or skill transfer needs. Look for people who are willing to learn, are eager to seek new skills or knowledge, are receptive to feedback and encouragement, and have the time to commit to the relationship.

In selecting mentors, look for individuals with the ability to encourage protégés, knowledge about the sought-after aspects of the operation and/or company, and the time to commit to the relationship. To be most effective, be sure your mentors have a significant depth of the skills and knowledge needed by the protégés and are willing to share their experiences.

7. Pair Mentors with Protégés. Pairing mentors with protégés is a critical step in any formal mentoring program. While there is no exact science for pairing people together, here are some tips to help you start:

- *Look for people who have complementary needs.* For example, a mentor who wants to give advice on leadership development would do well with a protégé who is looking for exactly that information.

- *Review work experience.* The most successful relationships are those when a gap of experience exists, with the mentor being more senior, the protégé more junior.

- *Attempt to pair people from similar fields.* For example, if the protégé is technical, an employee who has some technical experience somewhere in his or her background would probably be a better match as the mentor.

- *Consider personality styles.* For example, a person who focuses solely on details may benefit from being paired with someone with a big-picture focus.

- *Think about work location.* While it's ideal to have the mentor and protégé in the same location, keep in mind that e-mail, teleconferencing, instant messaging, and voicemail can all prove to be successful vehicles for mentoring when properly utilized. (See Exhibit 15.3.)

- *Consider responsibility level.* You may want to select protégés from a consistent responsibility level within the organization, that is, middle managers or succession candidates.

8. Orient/Train Mentors and Protégés. While Molly knew she needed help and Jeri knew how to provide it, that's not always the case. A mentoring contract and an orientation or training session that describes roles, responsibilities, how to create an effective relationship, and expectations of the program are beneficial to any mentoring program. One training session can be held for all mentoring program participants or, as is done at Microsoft (which has an effective formal mentoring program in place), you can hold separate training sessions for mentors and protégés. This allows members of either group to feel free to ask questions about their responsibilities as well as what they can expect from their partners.

The orientation and training can be done in person or by using any of the e-learning training methods available. A thorough orientation and training typically runs four to eight hours in length. See the sample mentoring topics list in Exhibit 15.4 and the orientation agenda in Exhibit 15.5.

9. **Develop the Mentoring Relationship.** Once the participants have been selected, paired, and trained, it's time for them to begin developing their relationships with their partners. The mentoring relationship takes time to develop, so be sure to tell participants to be patient. The mentor and protégé have to get acquainted and discuss guidelines before they can establish goals and develop a trusting relationship. Some sample mentor and protégé guidelines are presented for your use (Exhibits 15.6 and 15.7). You may wish to have the mentoring pairs complete contracts like the sample shown in Exhibit 15.8 to agree on what their relationship will be. Be sure that the coordinator is accessible during this time, should any questions or problems arise.

10. **Track Progress.** To ensure that the mentoring relationships have been established and that protégés are achieving their learning objectives, it's important for the program coordinator to periodically check in with the pairs. Progress can be tracked through the use of a survey, a group meeting, or individual contact with each mentor and protégé. You'll want to check in more frequently at the start of a program (at least once a month) to ensure the program is off to a good start. Quarterly check-ins are sufficient once you determine the program is on track.

Phase III: Evaluate

11. **Distribute Surveys to Participants and Analyze Results.** As with any training method, it's important to measure its success. The most common way of evaluating the success of a mentoring program is by surveying the participants. Response rates are improved by distributing the evaluation in person. This can be done at a final meeting (graduation) of the mentors and protégés. A sample evaluation is provided in Exhibit 15.9 at the end of this chapter.

Depending on the purpose of the program, other measures may help to evaluate the program's effectiveness. For example, if the program was designed to train program managers to expedite the introduction of new products on the manufacturing floor, a measure of new product introduction time before and after the program was implemented can be used as an indicator of success.

12. Determine Whether the Program Will Continue. Use the results of the evaluation and determine whether needs still exist in the organization for a transfer of knowledge from more-experienced to less-experienced employees. If the answer is yes, decide whether or not to continue the mentoring program.

How to Blend Mentoring with Classroom Training

While mentoring is most often combined with classroom training in an informal manner, there are numerous ways it can be more formally paired with an instructor-led class. The various ways to combine the two include:

- Pair a less-experienced participant with a more-experienced participant from the same class.

- Pair a recent participant with someone who took the class previously and has more experience in applying the class content.

- Pair the participants with the class instructor(s).

- Have the participants serve as mentors to people who have not taken the class. This gives the participants the responsibility to teach someone else what they have learned, which is the most effective way to thoroughly absorb new skills and knowledge.

See Chapters 5 through 7 for additional information on how to blend training solutions.

KEY POINTS

- The greater the number of learners, the more likely it is that the organization would benefit from a formal mentoring program instead of an informal mentoring program.

- Use communication channels to prepare the entire organization for your mentoring program.

- Pair mentors and protégés carefully.

- Both mentors and protégés have to be trained or oriented to understand their roles and to ensure valuable relationships are formed.

- Follow up on mentoring pairs to make sure the relationships thrive.

RESOURCES

Kaye, B., & Scheef, D. (2000). *Mentoring.* Alexandria, VA: ASTD. Describes types of mentoring and covers mentoring myths, guidelines, and "do's" and "don'ts."

Klasen, N., & Clutterbuck, D. (2001). *Implementing mentoring schemes: A practical guide to successful programs.* London: Butterworth-Heinemann. A practical, comprehensive, "how-to" guide on the design, implementation, and evaluation of mentoring programs.

Stromei, L. K., & Phillips, J. (Eds.). (2001). *In action: Creating mentoring and coaching programs.* Alexandria, VA: ASTD. Twelve cases that demonstrate a variety of mentoring and coaching programs in various work settings.

Thomas, S. J., & Douglas, P. J. (2004). *Structured mentoring: A new approach that works.* Alexandria, VA: ASTD. A basic guide on how to use mentoring to improve performance, increase retention, and jump-start projects.

Exhibit 15.1. Sample Executive Summary.

What Is Mentoring?

Mentoring is a work-related partnership—grounded in development—between two people that allows an individual with more experience (the mentor) to share skills, knowledge, and experience with an individual with less experience (the mentee or protégé). A mentor is a tutor, a role model, and a teacher. Done properly, mentoring provides opportunities for individuals to grow and learn in a helpful, responsive environment.

Our Business Case for Mentoring

Several conditions support the need for mentoring in our organization. [Bullet the key conditions, such as need for skills transition, building leadership bench strength, and others.]

- Condition 1:
- Condition 2:

How Can Mentoring Help?

- Many executives find mentoring to be an important development tool, and it has played a key role in the personal career success of several.
- Mentoring is used by many successful organizations, such as Accenture, Ernst & Young, Deloitte Touche, Microsoft, and Motorola.
- Numerous U.S. companies have implemented mentoring programs and have found that mentoring is effective in the retention and improved performance of employees.

What's the Investment?

The investment required to implement a mentoring program is primarily time—the time commitment required by both the mentor and protégé. Participants are asked to meet [frequency of meeting] for [time frame of meetings]. In addition, participants will be asked to attend an orientation and training session that will require [number of hours] of their time. The mentoring program will run for [time length].

Exhibit 15.1. Sample Executive Summary, *Continued.*

Who's Involved?

[Name] is the program coordinator. He/She will be leading the selection and training of participants and will monitor and evaluate the program's success. In addition, [number] candidates will be serving as mentors and protégés.

What's Needed from You?

Support. It's important to the success of the program that you communicate your knowledge of this program and that you demonstrate your support by giving participants permission to take the time to be involved.

Exhibit 15.2. Sample Communication Describing Mentoring.

Background

Mentoring is a partnership between two people, where the individual with more experience (the mentor) is asked to share skills, knowledge, and experience with an individual with less experience (the mentee or protégé). We are implementing a mentoring program in our organization to help address these business conditions: [List the two to three key conditions used in your Executive Summary.]

- Condition 1:
- Condition 2:
- Condition 3:

Goals of Mentoring

By implementing mentoring in our organization, we expect to achieve the following goals: [List the goals for your mentoring program.]

- Goal:
- Goal:
- Goal:

Target Population

Mentoring will be implemented for [enter the target population]. Participants will be selected by [enter your selection method, for example, nominations, applications].

Time Frame

This project will begin on [insert date] and will be completed by [insert date].

Project Coordinator and Responsibilities

[Project coordinator] will be responsible for leading the project. She/he will be responsible for overseeing the selection of participants and their training, as well as monitoring and evaluating the program.

For More Information

If you have any questions, don't hesitate to contact me at [include name and contact information].

**Exhibit 15.3. Sample Handout for Mentoring Relationship
with Pairs at Two Different Locations.**

In today's fast-moving work environment, it can be difficult to find time to establish and build a mentoring relationship. The increasing acceptance of e-mail as a form of communication has made finding time a little easier.

Advantages

- E-mail allows the mentor and protégé to be in different locations and still maintain a relationship.

- Each of you can select the most appropriate time to read and respond to your mentoring e-mails.

Tips

- Keep in mind that, since e-mail is text-based, it may not convey many of the messages that are contained in non-verbal communication (how you say something, rather than what you say).

- Make sure both parties are equally computer literate before starting an e-mail mentoring relationship.

- Remember that there is a time delay between sending and receiving and reading e-mails.

- Supplement e-mails with phone contact when possible.

Exhibit 15.4. Sample Mentoring Topics.

- Clarify which new skills or knowledge has to be learned.
- Discuss the best way to learn the new skills or gain the knowledge.
- Talk about how and when to apply new skills or knowledge.
- Obtain ideas about how to prepare to take on new responsibilities.
- Ask for suggestions on how to advance your career.
- Obtain suggestions about how to "work within the system."
- Find out about jobs in other departments.
- Ask about how to balance corporate expectations with your own.
- Talk about stress and time management.

Exhibit 15.5. Sample Mentoring Orientation Agenda.

30 minutes	Introductions
30 minutes	Purpose of the mentoring program
1 hour	Program guidelines
	• Length
	• Frequency of contact
	• Expenses
15 minutes	Break
1 hour	Roles and responsibilities
	• Coordinator
	• Mentors
	• Protégés
1 hour	Lunch with partners
1 hour, 20 minutes	Communication tips
30 minutes	Resources available to participants
20 minutes	Future group meetings

Exhibit 15.6. Sample Mentor Guidelines.

- Be the one who initiates contact (both at the beginning and later, if you haven't heard from your protégé for a while).

- Suggest topics to discuss, and ask what your protégé's needs are.

- Be explicit about your limits.

- Keep your discussions confidential.

- Listen to your protégé respectfully.

- State explicitly that you are only making suggestions, and do not be offended if your protégé chooses not to take your advice.

- Let your protégé know that he or she may well receive conflicting advice from different people and that it is his or her responsibility to make decisions.

- Be encouraging. Share stories of your own and others' successes and recognize your protégé's successes.

- Be honest in your advice—don't be afraid to offer critical feedback. When criticism is offered, follow it with constructive advice for improvement.

- Review the mentoring agreement with your partner regularly, and make any changes you think are necessary.

Exhibit 15.7. Sample Protégé Guidelines.

- Be specific when asking for advice. Do not assume that advice will be offered if it is not solicited.

- Be considerate of your mentor's time. Respond promptly to phone or e-mail messages.

- Show appreciation for the time and assistance given to you by your mentor.

- Keep your discussions confidential.

- Pay attention to what your mentor has to say. Although some information may seem irrelevant to you, it may prove useful in the future.

- Review the mentoring agreement with your partner regularly, and make any changes you think are necessary.

- If your mentoring partnership doesn't seem to be working out, address the issues with your mentor first. If you are unable to resolve the issues, then contact the mentoring coordinator.

Exhibit 15.8. Sample Mentoring Contract.

The following contract is a critical part of your first discussion. The process of writing, clarifying, and agreeing on expectations has proven to be one of the most valuable and powerful tools for helping mentoring relationships to be mutually satisfying.

Process: The protégé should complete items 1 and 2 and bring this form to the first meeting. Collectively, the mentor and protégé should complete the remainder of the form and both should sign and keep a copy.

Protégé: _____   Mentor: _____

1. As a protégé, my focus is on (skills to be developed):

2. At the completion of this mentoring program, I will be able to (do, know, demonstrate):

3. Specific activities to help accomplish these goals are:

4. Frequency and length of meetings will be:

5. [Name] will schedule the meetings.

6. Ground rules for our relationship include (for example, confidentiality, rescheduling meetings):

Other comments or concerns:

_____ _____   _____ _____
Protégé signature   Date   Mentor signature   Date

The Other Blended Learning. Copyright © 2005 by John Wiley & Sons, Inc. Reproduced by permission of Pfeiffer, an Imprint of Wiley. www.pfeiffer.com

Exhibit 15.9. Sample Evaluation Form.

Instructions: Please respond to the following questions, which are meant to:

- Measure your satisfaction with the mentoring program
- Evaluate the effectiveness of the program

Your responses will be completely confidential. Please complete and return this form to [coordinator] by [date].

Were you a _____ mentor or a _____ protégé?

What was your satisfaction with the initial training/orientation you received?

_____ Excellent   _____ Good   _____ Average   _____ Fair   _____ Poor

How frequently did you meet with your protégé/mentor?

_____ More than once per month

_____ Once per month

_____ Less than once per month

Were clear learning goals established for the relationship?

_____ Yes   _____ No

Were the learning goals achieved?

_____ Not at all   _____ Somewhat   _____ Completely

How would you rate your overall satisfaction level with your mentoring relationship?

_____ Excellent   _____ Good   _____ Average   _____ Fair   _____ Poor

Comments:

16

Coaching

Tom was irritated. His boss was pressing him to take advantage of the coaching program the company just set up. It wasn't enough that he took the time to go to the manager training, now she wanted him to waste even more time meeting with some coach to help be a better manager. Did she want him to get his job done or didn't she? He'd agreed to do it, but only because he had to—it still would be a waste of time and money.

Tom met with a coach a week later, still feeling irritated. His first impression didn't do much to change his opinion; Susan, his coach, had a human resources background, not a technical one. How could she help him to better manage a bunch of engineers? He was surprised when she explained that she wasn't there to tell him how to be a better manager and that he already had the knowledge he needed. Instead, she explained, she was there to help him figure out the reason he wasn't applying what he knew, to look within himself for the answers. Tom groaned inwardly—it was even worse than he thought it would be.

He reluctantly agreed to meet for twelve weeks, keeping his boss's good graces in mind. And at least Susan wasn't telling him he didn't know how to do his job. A few weeks went by, and in each session Susan gently persisted in asking him about his beliefs about his employees and their capabilities, what he thought his strengths and weaknesses were, and what he thought of the material from the manager training he had attended. She never criticized him for any of his answers; she really did seem to believe that he was a capable manager.

Much to his surprise, Tom began to realize that he didn't believe his employees were capable of doing a good job at all, and certainly not able to do things as well as he could. He had never really thought about it before; he had always told them they were doing a good job (he knew enough about managing people to do that), but he realized that he hadn't really meant it. He also realized that, when it came right down to it, they probably knew perfectly well he didn't mean it. When Susan asked him how he would feel if he were in their shoes, the answer was obvious. He would feel talked down to, resentful, and most definitely not motivated to do a good job.

At no point did Susan judge him for any of this, and she had every reason to, he thought to himself. She always treated him with respect, as though everything he had done up to this point was for a valid reason. He relaxed and began to try the different methods he had learned in the class, only this time giving them a real chance. He tried a variety of things and used the coaching sessions with Susan to review how well they worked. Some methods he never felt comfortable with, and so he set them aside. Others worked quite well, and he began to incorporate them almost unconsciously into his daily routine. Eventually he realized that Susan had been right from the very beginning; he already knew what he needed to do to be a good manager. And for the first time, he was actually doing it.

What Is Coaching?

Most people are familiar with the idea of coaching as it is used in sports, where a coach assists an athlete to gain new skills in order to improve his or her performance. Life and career coaching, on the other hand, presume that participants already possess the knowledge and skills they need but for some reason are not applying them. The International Coach Federation (ICF) defines this type of coaching as "an ongoing relationship, which focuses on clients taking action toward the realization of their visions, goals, or desires. Coaching uses a process of inquiry and personal discovery to build the client's level of awareness and responsibility and provides the client with structure, support, and feedback. The coaching process helps clients both define and achieve professional and personal goals faster and with more ease than would be possible otherwise."

The ICF adds that coaches are "trained to listen, to observe, and to customize their approach to individual client needs. They seek to elicit solutions and strategies from the client; they believe the client is naturally creative and resourceful. The coach's job is to provide support to enhance the skills, resources, and creativity that the client already has" (International Coach Federation, 2000). Coaching is a rapidly growing field; in 2003 there were twenty thousand coaches practicing worldwide, with almost three-quarters of them in the United States.

While coaching is frequently used to help individuals achieve personal goals, it can also be used as a training solution to enhance goals, knowledge, and skills applicable to organizations. Coaching is, however, a significantly different approach from other training techniques, which generally focus on providing opportunities for participants to gain new knowledge and skills. Since the clients are presumed to already possess the needed knowledge and skills, the coach's job is to ask them to examine reasons for their behaviors and to guide them in identifying the internal obstacles, old beliefs, or patterns of thinking that can prevent them from changing their behavior. The purpose of doing so is to acknowledge the obstacle—whatever it may be—and provide participants with a choice of whether to continue with the old pattern or work to adopt the new.

Although similar in structure, coaching is very different from mentoring. In mentoring, one person is clearly identified as the expert from whom the other person is to learn new skills, knowledge, or information; the relationship is hierarchical in nature. In coaching, on the other hand, the coach provides *support* for the client's goals, and the relationship is much more of a partnership. The coach's role is not that of an expert or authority.

The coaching field encompasses a wide variety of specialty areas such as personal development, career development, spirituality, relationships, and recovery. Since this book focuses on using coaching in a blended learning context, we limited our discussion to only those areas where coaching is most often used to enhance learning. In the business world, three kinds of coaching are generally used in this context. They include:

- *Executive coaching*—Often the skills required to move people into executive positions are not the ones needed to keep them there. Executives most often need help using leadership, decision making, strategic planning, and visioning skills.

- *Managerial coaching*—Many managers are highly technical people who have moved into management roles due to their technical expertise. They often lack even basic managerial skills, and coaching can be enormously helpful after other training methods have provided basic information. Often managers who have been trained in management theories and skills face difficulty in the actual implementation and in behavioral change. Managers often seek coaches to help them develop their skills in motivation, productivity, teamwork, interpersonal communication skills, and goal setting.

- *Career coaching*—Employees at all levels of organizations benefit from career coaching, where they receive help in identifying and pursuing their career goals as well as applying specific skills such as market research, networking, interviewing, and negotiating.

Some pros and cons of using coaching are listed below.

Pros
- Is focused on the participants' perspective, so they are often highly motivated;
- Provides one-on-one attention and support; and
- Is flexible and can be used both in person and over the telephone.

Cons

- Can be an expensive option;

- Requires specialized skills; and

- Can be used inappropriately as therapy or consulting, if the coach isn't adequately trained.

When to Use Coaching

Coaching is most effective when two conditions exist. The first is that the participants already have the knowledge or skills needed to change their behaviors. If they don't, we suggest offering another solution such as classroom training or mentoring first to provide the necessary knowledge or skills; then blend it with coaching to turn the learning into actual behavioral change.

The second condition is that each participant be willing to do honest introspection and be willing to take responsibility for his or her actions and decisions. If Tom had continued to blame his employees for their lack of motivation or his boss for forcing him to attend coaching sessions, then the coaching sessions would indeed have been a waste of time. Coaching takes the approach that you can't force someone to take this responsibility; you can only encourage him or her to take it. This can be difficult to determine ahead of time; often the only way to see whether coaching will be a helpful solution is to try it and see. You can usually tell within one or two sessions whether the participant is willing to do the work; and, if not, continuing the sessions will be wasteful.

Coaching in the business world is most often used for traditional soft skills such as interpersonal communication, managerial skills, decision making, productivity, and strategic planning.

How to Implement Coaching

Coaching can be provided either by external coaches or by internal resources. This is changing, as the field is growing rapidly, but at present, it is more common to hire external coaches rather than develop coaching expertise internally.

Keep in mind that, to be most effective, coaching is used when the participants already have the knowledge or skills they need but are not applying them. This is significantly different from other training solutions. For example, a manager may have been trained in effective meeting techniques but continues to run meetings that start late, run long, and never have agendas. If employees don't already possess the needed knowledge or skills, coaching is an excellent solution to implement following another method such as classroom training or mentoring. Use the following steps to implement a coaching program:

1. Determine whether external or internal coaches will be used.
2. Determine the time frame and structure of the coaching relationships.
3. Obtain management support for the program.
4. Invite or select participants.
5. Implement the coaching relationship(s).
6. Evaluate and analyze results.

1. Determine Whether External or Internal Coaches Will Be Used

You must first determine whether people within the organization have the time and skills to successfully deliver coaching. Since coaching is such a new field, skill levels and credentialing vary widely. Coaching requires a skill set that is different from those of classroom and other training solutions; the primary skills necessary for successful coaching are listening, questioning, and empathizing.

Listening. A critical skill used in coaching is listening. While listening is a key skill in other training methods, the emphasis is far greater in coaching. In classroom training, for example, presentation skills are as important as listening skills. But in coaching, presentation skills are much less important than the ability to hear clearly and effectively without bias or judgment.

Questioning. Questioning skills are also critical to successful coaching. Because coaches believe that participants already have the necessary skills and knowledge, they need highly developed questioning skills to draw these out, to enhance the creativity already existing within the participants, and to identify any obstacles the participants may have placed in the way of implementing new skills or behaviors. Effective coaches must be able to probe deeply and respectfully. As in the example at the beginning of the chapter, Tom had already learned what he needed to do to be a better manager but still wasn't successful in implementing those new skills. It took Susan's thoughtful questions for him to realize that the barriers to his success were due to his subconscious beliefs. Once he identified the barriers, then he realized they were entirely within his power to change, if he chose to do so.

Empathy. A third essential skill a coach needs is that of empathy, the ability to identify with and understand another person's situation, feelings, and motives. Coaching asks participants to look within themselves rather than to acquire new knowledge or skills; this can be frightening for most people, sometimes enormously so. Without empathy on the part of the coach, trust can be difficult to establish; and without trust, people simply will not open themselves to introspection. Empathy is extremely difficult to learn, so when you select someone as a coach, this skill requires the closest scrutiny.

2. Determine the Time Frame and Structure of the Coaching Relationships

In the business world, coaching can be conducted in individual, face-to-face sessions or it can be conducted over the telephone or via e-mail. The decision of which approach to use depends on the physical location of the coach and participant, their style preferences, and the business practices of both the coach and the organization. The coach and client usually schedule a series of meetings, often meeting weekly or biweekly. The duration and number of the sessions vary widely, generally lasting from half an hour to an hour in length and usually from a few months to a year in time span, with three months as a minimum. The first session is directed by the coach and usually focuses on introductory topics such as:

- The client's goals for the coaching relationship. While goals tend to change, initial goals are helpful in beginning the coaching process.

- The frequency and duration of the coaching sessions.
- The client's expectations of the coaching process.

A sample agenda for a first coaching session is shown in Exhibit 16.1. The actual coaching usually begins during the second session. This session, as well as subsequent sessions, is generally directed by the client, with the coach interjecting questions and comments only when needed. A sample coaching agreement is presented in Exhibit 16.2 at the end of this chapter.

3. Obtain Management Support for the Program

Obtaining upper management support for a coaching program is essential due to the potential financial and human resource requirements needed to implement it. Coaching can be an expensive solution, since it most often is delivered one-on-one. Additionally, coaching can take a significant amount of time, depending on the duration of the coaching relationship(s).

4. Invite or Select Participants

Determine who might benefit from coaching and decide whether you will allow people to self-select for the program or whether you will take manager nominations or appointments. As was mentioned above, look for participants who already have skills (or who will have them once other training solutions have been provided) and those who are willing to do honest introspection and are willing to take responsibility for their actions and decisions.

Selecting coaches for participants is a critical and sometimes difficult step, since there is no exact science for pairing people together. You can simply assign coaches to participants or, if you have the flexibility to do so, allow participants to interview and select their own coaches (from the world at large or from a list of coaches you've already screened and approved). The second option will typically be more effective; since coaching tends to be a personal relationship, allowing an individual to select his or her own coach greatly improves the chances that the coach will be a good fit.

5. Implement the Coaching Relationship(s)

Once all of the preparation has been completed, the coaching relationship actually begins. As with mentoring, coaching relationships take time to develop, so you may want to advise the participants to be patient. If you are using external coaches, make arrangements for the first meetings with the participants. Arrangements for future coaching sessions should be made during the first meeting.

If you are the coach, use the initial coaching meeting to get to know the client and to establish the "ground rules" of the relationship; the sessions beyond the first one are used to accomplish the real work of the coaching relationship.

As you build the relationship, use questions to elicit the reasons why your client is not using the skills or knowledge he or she already has. The most helpful questions used in coaching focus on the "what" or the "how." As a coach, your job is to assist clients in identifying what they know, feel, or believe as well as how they can change their behavior, their feelings, or their beliefs.

Use any questions beginning with "why" very carefully. Coaches are not typically qualified to be therapists, and often "why" questions are directed at underlying issues, many of which are best left to psychological professionals. It didn't matter why Tom believed he was more capable than his employees; it was enough for him to identify that he did indeed harbor that belief and that continuing to do so impacted his ability to effectively motivate those who worked for him. One of the distinctions between therapy and coaching can be defined in terms of time: A therapist focuses primarily on the past, while a coach focuses primarily on the present and future.

Samples of helpful coaching questions include:

- What keeps you from getting the results you want?
- How can you address this situation? What have you tried already?
- What worked for you in previous situations?
- How do you think people view your management style?
- If you did know the answer, what would it be?

As a coach, listen carefully to what is being said, as well as to what is not being said, and draw out any feelings or ideas that you suspect are not spoken. Some of the clues to watch for include:

- Tone of voice (excited, happy, resigned, complaining);
- Amount of enthusiasm when discussing any particular topic;
- Choice of words used;
- Level of anxiety;
- Body language (if in person);
- Perceived strengths;
- Perceived weaknesses;
- Values; and
- Disconnects between what is said and the actions being taken.

Listen without judgment or filters; the agenda in coaching comes from the client, not from you. Your role as a coach is to provide structure, support, and feedback, not expertise; what matters in the relationship is the client's thoughts and feelings, not yours. This is significantly different from the role of a consultant and from that of other training professionals. Rid yourself of any internal discussions or distractions in order to focus completely on the client's needs.

Finally, be comfortable with silence in the relationship. Our culture encourages us to fill silence as quickly as possible, but leaving a comfortable, open space for your client to process information is one of the most powerful listening skills you can master. To test your ability, take a watch with a second hand the next time you are talking with someone. Allow at least seven seconds to pass in silence while you wait for a reply. If you can learn to do this comfortably in coaching sessions, you will provide the time and space your clients need to fully process their thoughts and responses to whatever was just said. Some additional tips for coaches are presented in Exhibit 16.3.

6. Evaluate and Analyze Results

As with any training method, it's important to measure success. The most common way of evaluating the success of a coaching program is by surveying the participants (Level 1 evaluation data). Since coaching is conducted with people who already have skills and knowledge, Level 2 evaluation is not generally useful. However, since the purpose of coaching is to move a client from knowledge to behavioral change, Level 3 evaluation data can be extremely helpful in determining the success of the coaching relationship. For example, if an employee is working on his or her effective meeting skills, you could observe meetings both before and after the coaching to see whether his or her behaviors have changed. Or you could use a 360-degree assessment instrument before and after a coaching relationship to see what changes, if any, a manager has made in his or her supervisory behaviors. We've provided sample Level 1 and 3 evaluation forms in Exhibits 16.4 and 16.5 at the end of this chapter.

How to Blend Coaching with Classroom Training

Coaching is an excellent complement to classroom training. New skills can be introduced and learned in the classroom setting, but real behavioral change often falls by the wayside as people return to the pressures of their jobs. Coaching can greatly increase the chance that the newly learned behaviors become part of the client's daily practice. As in our example, Tom had already learned what he needed to do to be a better manager. Susan's coaching allowed him to do three things: (1) to identify how much he was resisting adopting the new behaviors; (2) to practice what he had learned; and (3) to receive feedback in a safe and supportive atmosphere.

See Chapters 5 through 7 for additional information on how to blend training solutions.

KEY POINTS

- Coaching is different from other training solutions in that it presumes that participants already possess the knowledge and skills they need but for some reason are not applying them.

- The skills required of an effective coach are also different from those needed for most other training solutions, so be sure to select your coaches carefully.

- Coaching is most helpful when two conditions exist: (1) the clients already have the skills and knowledge they need and (2) they are willing to do honest introspection and to take responsibility for their actions and decisions.

RESOURCES

Fairley, S. G., & Stout, C. E. (2003). *Getting started in personal and executive coaching: How to create a thriving coaching practice.* Hoboken, NJ: John Wiley & Sons. A go-to reference designed to help every mental health professional build, manage, and sustain a thriving coaching practice.

International Coach Federation. (2000). *The language/distinctions document: Parameters of coaching.*

Leonard, T. J. (1998). *The portable coach: 28 surefire strategies for business and personal success.* New York: Charles Scribner. A practical guide to attracting personal and business success; includes steps and self-testing materials that can be used for coaching others or oneself.

Martin, C. (2001). *The life coaching handbook: Everything you need to become an effective life coach.* Williston, VT: Crown House Publishing. A guide that defines what life coaching is and how to create and sustain a successful coaching practice; includes NLP-based techniques.

Neenan, M., & Dryden, W. (2002). *Life coaching: A cognitive behavioural approach.* New York: Taylor & Francis, Inc. A handbook showing how to tackle self-defeating thinking and replace it with a problem-solving outlook.

Exhibit 16.1. Sample Agenda for a First Coaching Session.

Use this agenda to guide you through the first coaching session. Keep in mind that you lead the first session but that all other subsequent sessions are dictated by the client's agenda, not yours.

Logistics

Confirm the following information:

- Meeting time, place, and frequency
- Payment process (if applicable)
- Coaching contract (if not already signed)

Introductions

- Briefly introduce yourself.
- Ask the client to tell you about himself/herself.

Goals and Intentions

- Ask what the client hopes to get out of the coaching.
- Ask him or her to commit to at least three goals for the next session.
- Assign an assessment, if appropriate.

Exhibit 16.2. Sample Coaching Agreement.

Welcome, Tom!

I appreciate the opportunity to work with you as your coach and am looking forward to our journey together. I'd like you to be familiar with the following policies and procedures. If you have any questions, please call.

Procedure: We will meet at your office once a week for approximately one hour. We have set your sessions to be on Tuesdays at 9:30 a.m. beginning on October 10.

Changes: If you need to reschedule your session, give me at least twenty-four hours' notice. If you have an emergency, we'll work around it. If you must cancel a meeting, we'll make it up so you will have four sessions in the month.

Extra time: You may call me in between your scheduled sessions if you need advice, have a problem, or can't wait to share a success. I do have time between our regular calls to speak with you if needed, and I enjoy providing this extra level of service. I do not bill for additional time of this type. I am available to you when you need me, although I do ask that you keep the extra calls to five or ten minutes.

Closure: Please give thirty days' notice when discontinuing our coaching relationship. This will give us ample time to complete projects, plan strategies for your future, and have closure as coach and client.

Problems: If I ever say or do something that upsets you or doesn't feel right, please bring it up. I promise to do what is necessary to satisfy you.

Liability (the small print): You understand that these sessions are consultative in nature and that any actions and decisions made by you are solely your responsibility. I am not a licensed therapist and coaching is not a substitute for professional therapy. The coach shall in no way be held liable or responsible for any actions taken, or not taken, by you. The coach makes no guarantees or warranties, expressed or implied, about any results to be achieved.

I understand the aforementioned and by signing this contract I agree to comply.

Please sign and return to me by fax at xxx-xxx-xxxx. Keep a copy for yourself. Welcome aboard!

_____   _____
Name of Coach   Date   Name of Client   Date

Source: With permission from Judy Irving PCC, Executive Coach. www.movingon.net

---

Exhibit 16.3. Sample Coaching Tips.

Use the tips below to make your coaching more effective.

Listen for what is not being said. Watch for clues such as:

- Tone of voice (excited, happy, resigned, complaining)

- Amount of enthusiasm when discussing any particular topic

- Choice of words used

- Level of anxiety

- Integrity

- Body language (if in person)

- Perceived strengths

- Perceived weaknesses

- Values

Use effective questions such as:

- What keeps you from getting the results you want?

- How can you address this situation? What have you tried already?

- What worked for you in previous situations?

- How do you think people view your management style?

- If you did know the answer, what would it be?

Keep yourself completely present. Ask yourself:

- What is he or she really saying?

- Am I hearing what he or she is saying or what I'm assuming he or she is saying?

- Am I thinking about what to have for dinner tonight?

Exhibit 16.4. Sample Level 1 Evaluation Form for Coaching.

Participant Evaluation Form

Instructions: Please rate the following on a scale of 1 to 4 by circling your choices.

1 = Strongly disagree; 2 = Unsure; 3 = Agree; 4 = Strongly agree

Goals   1   2   3   4

I generally reached all of the weekly goals that I set for myself.

Comments: _____

Accessibility   1   2   3   4

My coach was easy to reach and available when I needed him or her.

Comments: _____

Sense of Trust   1   2   3   4

I felt very comfortable with my coach and always felt she or he had my best interests
at heart.

Comments: _____

Satisfaction   1   2   3   4

I feel satisfied with my coaching experience.

Comments: _____

Recommendation   1   2   3   4

I would recommend coaching to other people who want to move more quickly toward
their personal and professional goals.

Comments: _____

Exhibit 16.5. Sample Level 3 Evaluation Form for Coaching.

Instructions: Use this evaluation form for observing behavioral change when coaching someone to more effectively schedule and conduct meetings.

Effective Meeting Checklist

Use the checklist below to determine how well a meeting was prepared and conducted.

	Yes	Somewhat	No
Preparing for the Meeting			
An agenda was sent out in advance.	☐	☐	☐
The agenda contained topics, estimated times, and purpose.	☐	☐	☐
Each item indicated whether it was a decision to be made or information only.	☐	☐	☐
The meeting place was scheduled in advance and clearly communicated.	☐	☐	☐
Conducting the Meeting			
The facilitator made sure everyone had a chance to contribute.	☐	☐	☐
No single person dominated the discussion.	☐	☐	☐
The meeting started on time.	☐	☐	☐
The meeting ended on time.	☐	☐	☐
Each agenda item was covered within its estimated time duration.	☐	☐	☐
Items requiring additional discussion were tabled and discussed later.	☐	☐	☐
Action items were documented, including who, what, and when.	☐	☐	☐

17

On-the-Job Training

Jerome was excited about his new job as a night manager for a boutique hotel. While he had worked for several years as a front desk clerk for a hotel chain, this was his first experience in management. He was going to be sharing the night manager duties with one other experienced manager, and he was starting at the same time as another new manager who had just joined the company. Jerome was very anxious to begin his new assignment and was surprised to learn of the extensive training program being offered. At his previous employer, he learned how to do his job by trial and error.

His training involved a comprehensive blended learning approach. He was sent materials to read about the hotel's history and customer service reputation prior to reporting to work the first day. His first three days on the job were spent in the classroom, learning about the hotel's values and culture and how to live them. Basic customer service training was also provided, and rules and regulations such as dress code and work hours were discussed.

Once the formal classroom training was concluded, Jerome and the other new manager were assigned to Erma, an experienced manager, who helped them learn more about how to perform their specific jobs. Erma gave the new managers a tour of the facilities so they would be familiar with the locations and functions of all of the other departments at the hotel, such as housekeeping and food service. The following day she asked them to show her where the various departments were located, so she could verify that they remembered what she had taught them.

Following the tour, they were taken to the front desk, where the clerk on duty demonstrated how he checked in customers, managed room key distribution, and collected payments when guests checked out. After watching these transactions, each new manager had to then perform the same transactions while the desk clerk observed and gave feedback. The next day was spent in food service, learning how food orders were received and filled. Jerome and his colleague assisted with the delivery of a food order to a meeting room. Friday was spent with the housekeeping manager, learning about the scheduling of housekeeping staff and the scheduling of rooms to be cleaned. The location of supplies and the procedure for requesting housekeeping services were covered as well.

On Monday before assuming their responsibilities as managers, Jerome and his colleague toured the maintenance department and had a chance to practice completing a work order and tracking its progress. At this point, they were both frustrated. "Why do we need to learn everyone else's jobs? We really just want to do our own." Erma explained that they would be on the job by the afternoon and suggested that once they assumed their roles as managers, it would be clear to them why they had participated in so much training.

Within the first four hours on the job, Jerome had to contact maintenance to get light bulbs replaced in a meeting room, and he received a call from an upset customer who had the wrong food delivered to her business meeting. All of the on-the-job training he had received prepared him to effectively and efficiently handle these situations with ease. "Ah, that's why they made me learn everyone else's jobs . . . so I can do mine!"

What Is On-the-Job Training?

On-the-job training (OJT) is job instruction that is conducted by having experienced employees train newer or less experienced employees at the actual work setting or in a setting that closely simulates the work setting. OJT can be structured or unstructured, and either type may be successfully blended with classroom training.

Unstructured OJT is where a more experienced employee may simply demonstrate how to complete a task for a less experienced employee. Unstructured OJT is useful for simple tasks such as demonstrating how to use interoffice mail or to expose someone to another task or job without providing detailed training. This type of on-the-job training is also known as job shadowing. Marriott International has a well-known job-shadowing program where high school students are introduced to the lodging industry by shadowing workers every Groundhog's Day.

Structured OJT involves one or more trainees and one or more trainers (more experienced employees) and a well-defined training process with learning objectives and evaluation tools in place. Jerome's experience at the hotel is an example of a structured on-the-job training program.

OJT is commonly used with employees who are new to an organization. Training on the use of company resources such as telephone systems and e-mail is frequently provided on the job. In addition, new graduates who are entering the workforce commonly have been introduced to theory, but need OJT to learn job-specific tasks.

Some of the pros and cons of on-the-job training are listed below.

Pros

- OJT provides opportunities for employees to learn the skills they need in the work setting where they will use them;

- Employees acquire new skills and knowledge at the same time they are actually performing some of their work responsibilities;

- Employees may feel more at ease being taught by someone they know rather than by classroom trainers; and

- OJT allows managers instant assessment of workers' learning progress.

Cons

- The work setting may be a distracting location for training;

- Workers conducting OJT may lack training expertise;

- OJT removes a skilled worker from his or her job while conducting the training; and

- Salary costs are often overlooked in calculating training costs.

When to Use On-the-Job Training

A mix of situations can benefit from OJT. For example, unstructured OJT is widely used with new employees. As part of a new hire's orientation, he or she is often trained by a more experienced employee on how to complete forms, use the copier, or use the voicemail system. A more structured OJT is most appropriate when:

- Smaller numbers of employees need to learn a hands-on skill;

- Experienced employees with the required skills are available to provide instruction; and/or

- Workstation(s) are available at which to conduct the training.

In determining whether or not to use OJT, consider both the nature of the work and the resources available. The nature of the work includes the type of work being performed, as well as its difficulty and frequency. An accountant would most likely not be able to learn mathematical skills through an on-the-job training program, but OJT could be an effective solution for a windshield installer. Skills that are manual, repetitive, non-complex, and applied consistently are ideal to teach in an on-the-job program.

Resources that have to be considered include the availability of experienced employees to conduct the training, the number and types of employees to be trained, training location and work distractions, and tools required to teach new tasks. For example, large numbers of bank employees learning a skill that requires them to practice on a computer or other equipment may not be practical, if it means fifteen people have to gather around one computer screen at a teller's window. However, if you have two new employees who have to learn how to operate a piece of equipment, having each one drive a forklift while the other one observes, for example, may be a very practical solution. In an open setting such as a manufacturing environment or an office environment with cubicles, it may be too distracting to other employees to have a group of trainees clustered nearby. For this reason, some larger organizations re-create the work setting in a classroom location near where the actual work is being done.

How to Implement On-the-Job Training

Once you have determined that a training need exists that can best be addressed by using OJT, decide whether you want to pursue a structured or unstructured OJT program. Unstructured programs are best to use when you only have one or two employees who need training and the training content is limited. Structured programs are typically best when you have three or more employees with a training need or when you want to repeat the training with other employees in the future.

An unstructured on-the-job training program can be implemented simply by pairing a more experienced employee with a less experienced employee to show him or her how to perform a job. Basically, the newer employee observes the more experienced employee as he or she goes about everyday work responsibilities. As always, in order to ensure that the training is effective, you should develop learning objectives and provide an opportunity for the learner to demonstrate that the skills or tasks were learned (this can be done through testing or demonstration). Once the need for a more structured program has been determined, implement it through the following steps:

1. Determine when to use.

2. Determine responsibilities.

3. Select and develop trainers.

4. Prepare materials.

5. Deliver training.

6. Evaluate/revise.

An outline of the process is shown in Exhibit 17.1 at the end of the chapter.

1. Determine When to Use

In addition to a needs assessment, OJT typically requires an analysis of the work to be done. The number of employees who need to learn the work will help determine whether OJT is the correct solution. Larger numbers of employees (more than seven) may be trained more efficiently in the classroom. Give consideration to the availability of expert employees to conduct the training as well as the availability of space in which to conduct the training.

2. Determine Responsibilities

Define roles prior to launching an OJT program. Determine who will conduct the training as well as who will develop the learning objectives, the modules to be taught, and the evaluation. If skilled employees will be removed from their work responsibilities while they conduct training, make arrangements for their work to be completed in their absence.

3. Select and Develop Trainers

The requirements for being an OJT trainer are similar to those for a subject-matter expert. These include the ability to treat others with respect, being known as an "answer person" (someone people naturally gravitate to when needing information), adequate content expertise, time available to prepare and conduct the training session, and support for the program from his or her manager. Senior managers should be involved in the selection of OJT trainers to ensure that the trainers' workload is lightened to allow them time to train. If the experienced employees you select to be OJT trainers do not possess these characteristics, we recommend that you have them participate in a train-the-trainer class. See the sample train-the-trainer blended solution provided in Exhibit 17.2 and Chapter 10, Subject-Matter Expert Training, for information on how to provide training skills to non-trainers. Additionally, consider providing incentives to employees to encourage their participation as trainers.

4. Prepare Materials

As with any training program, training objectives are the starting point of an OJT program. The amount and type of work to be taught will determine whether you will have one or many training modules. Resources such as equipment and materials have to be acquired, and content has to be developed. The training department and/or the instructional designer can do all of this, or an external expert can work with an internal subject-matter expert to design content.

5. Deliver Training

Once roles are determined, trainees and trainers have been identified, and the training materials have been prepared, it's time to present the content. Include a mix of explanation, demonstration, and practice. Trainers should provide immediate feedback to participants following their practice of a skill. It's also particularly important to include performance tests to ensure that entry-level content has been learned before moving on to more advanced content. Provide support to the OJT trainers throughout the process. A sample agenda is shown in Exhibit 17.3.

6. Evaluate/Revise

The final step is to evaluate. With on-the-job training, two elements should be evaluated: the program itself and to what extent the learning was successful. An evaluation of the program helps to determine whether the roles, trainers, and setting were satisfactory. Evaluation of the learning determines whether the learning objectives were met.

Include an assessment of roles in the program evaluation to determine whether responsibilities were appropriately assigned. Additionally, evaluate the employees who conducted the training, so that feedback can be given to them to help them improve their training skills. We also recommend obtaining feedback on the organization of the course content as well as the location of the training in order to determine its effectiveness (for example, there may be too many distractions in an actual job setting, or a simulated job setting may not be real enough). All of the feedback received should be taken into consideration in making revisions to the program. See the sample program evaluation in Exhibit 17.4 at the end of this chapter.

The learning can be evaluated by the use of any of the four levels discussed in Chapter 8, "Measure the Results of the Program." Because of the nature of an OJT program, the distinctions between Level 2 and Level 3 evaluations tend to blur. If learners demonstrate their ability to perform tasks in an on-the-job classroom, they are in fact demonstrating the application of that skill on their actual jobs. Scatter opportunities to demonstrate knowledge gained throughout the program in order to gather the most accurate feedback possible. See the sample learning evaluation form in Exhibit 17.5.

How to Blend On-the-Job Training with Classroom Training

Many organizations already use some form of OJT to train their employees in an unstructured manner. If you identify additional content to be delivered through OJT, there are various ways to integrate structured OJT with classroom training.

OJT is often interspersed with classroom training. A new skill or information can be taught in the classroom; then employees take that knowledge to their actual work settings and practice using it, while receiving feedback and support from more experienced employees. This blended approach is commonly used in customer service/call center settings, where basic information is taught in the classroom, followed by employees going into the call center and responding to actual customer calls while an "expert" listens in and ensures correct information is given to the customer. This approach ensures that what the employee learns in the classroom is transferred effectively to the work setting.

One of the most common combinations is to conduct classroom training covering basic or general information and follow up with OJT to teach specifics, as was demonstrated by Jerome's case at the beginning of this chapter. You may also start employees with OJT to teach them the basics about their jobs and then move them into the classroom to learn more advanced skills or to learn more about the rest of the organization.

Some organizations use OJT for cross-training purposes. In manufacturing, if employees already have basic assembly skills but have to be redeployed from one product line to another, OJT can be used effectively to teach them how to assemble a different product.

On-the-job training is frequently paired with job aids, as the type of work that lends itself to OJT also lends itself to job aids. For example, if an assembler is learning to build a new product, he or she may learn at the workstation, but would also have a step-by-step guide available to ensure consistency. See Chapters 5 through 7 for additional information on how to blend training solutions.

KEY POINTS

- OJT offers the opportunity for employees to learn new skills in the location at which they will be using those skills.

- OJT instructors should be carefully selected and be fully prepared with instructional skills.

- Training goals and objectives will keep your OJT program focused on the business need.

- Evaluation should be conducted throughout an OJT program to ensure that learners are gaining the desired skills.

RESOURCES

Jacobs, R. L. (2003). *Structured on-the-job training: Unleashing employee expertise into the workplace.* San Francisco, CA: Berrett-Koehler. A practical guide to understanding and using structured on-the-job training.

Rothwell, W. J., & Kazanas, H. C. (1994). *Improving on-the-job training.* San Francisco, CA: Pfeiffer. A complete, step-by-step guide to establishing or improving a comprehensive on-the-job training program.

Walter, D. (2001). *Training on the job.* Alexandria, VA: ASTD. A step-by-step guide to setting up a structured team-driven, on-the-job training program; includes templates, instructions, and checklists.

Exhibit 17.1. Sample OJT Project Plan.

Determine Responsibilities

Who will assign trainees?

Who will conduct training?

Who will prepare training materials?

Trainer Preparation

Select trainers.

Contact trainers' managers for permission to use them as trainers.

Notify trainers.

Conduct train-the-trainer sessions.

Prepare Materials

Determine training objectives.

Acquire resources (space for training, equipment, and so forth).

Design modules, including evaluation components.

Create handouts.

Deliver Training

Pilot if time allows.

Evaluate as you go.

Evaluate/Revise Training Program

Ask for participant feedback on the program.

Measure on-the-job effectiveness.

Make changes as warranted.

Exhibit 17.2. Sample Train-the-Trainer Blended Solution.

Topic and Duration/Timing	Key Points	Training Solution
Introduction to TTT (One month prior to classroom session)	• Introductions • Agenda and expectations • Introduction to adult learning principles (detailed TBTs to follow) • ADDIE Model (detailed TBTs to follow)	Instructor-led webinar
Basics of TTT (Sent following initial webinar session)	• Adult learning principles (link to online TBT) • ADDIE (link to online TBT)	E-mail post-work
Needs Assessment (Three weeks prior to classroom)	• Q&A from adult learning principles and ADDIE content (follow-up) • Needs assessment • Information to gather overview (form to be sent/completed) • Analyze the components overview (form to be sent/completed) • Wrap-up and expectations for follow-up items	Instructor-led webinar
Needs Assessment (Following second webinar)	• Form to be completed: Information to gather • Form to be completed: Components to analyze	E-mail post-work
Goals and Objectives and Training Materials (Three weeks prior)	• Q&A from needs assessment forms • Write a training goal overview (form to be sent/completed) • Write specific objectives overview (form to be sent/completed)	Instructor-led webinar

(continued)

Exhibit 17.2. Sample Train-the-Trainer Blended Solution, *Continued.*

Topic and Duration/Timing	Key Points	Training Solution
	• Research and organize content information • Training methods overview • Design/develop training materials (forms to be sent/completed)	
Goals and Objectives and Training Materials (Following third webinar)	• Form to be completed: Training goals and objectives • Materials to be edited: Sample training materials	E-mail post-work
Review Goals and Objectives and Training Materials (One week prior)	• Q&A from training goals and objectives • Review and questions from training materials • Wrap-up and preview	Conference call
Facilitation Skills	• Build rapport with the learners • Observe and react • Listen carefully • Ask effective questions	Classroom training session
Bringing It All Together	• Review of training agendas, methods, and materials • Evaluation	Classroom training session
Preparation for End-User Training (One week prior to the classroom session)	• Questions from classroom session • Questions in preparation of the end-user training	Conference call discussion
Evaluation Results (One week after the end-user training)	• Discussion of evaluation results	Conference call discussion

Exhibit 17.3. Sample OJT Agenda.

Hotel Orientation

Day 1

Amy: tour grounds

Bill: tour housekeeping

Wayne: tour maintenance

Sara: tour food service

Supervisor: meet key personnel, introduce to responsibilities

Day 2

Test for knowledge of department locations: have trainees demonstrate knowledge of location of head groundskeeper, housekeeping supervisor, maintenance director, and food service manager.

Work front desk: demonstrate and test for knowledge on guest check-in, guest check-out, handling customer complaints.

Day 3

Work food service: demonstrate and test for knowledge on guest room food order and meeting room food order.

Work maintenance: demonstrate and test for knowledge on taking/assigning/closing out maintenance requests.

Exhibit 17.4. Sample OJT Program Evaluation.

Instructions: Administer this evaluation to those individuals who were responsible for conducting the training, as well as those who were impacted by the training (for example, supervisors who had employees conducting the training or who had employees in the training).

1. Were roles and responsibilities clear?

   Comments:

2. Were managers appropriately informed?

   Comments:

3. Were the trainers well prepared?

   Comments:

4. Was the location of the training effective (not too loud, too disruptive, and so forth)?

   Comments:

Exhibit 17.5. Sample Learning Evaluation.

Instructions: Use the following scale to rate your learning experience. Then please offer your comments and suggestions on the program below.

Scale: 1 = Not at all   5 = Excellent

How would you rate your ability to perform the task   1 2 3 4 5
prior to the training?

How would you rate your ability to perform the task   1 2 3 4 5
following the training?

How comfortable are you that you can apply what   1 2 3 4 5
you learned in the future?

Did the trainer deliver the information in a clear, concise manner?   Yes   No

Comments:

Suggestions to improve the training program:

PART 3

Sample Designs Converting Classroom Training to Blended Learning

While some of you will be building a training program from start to finish, many of you already have training programs in place that could benefit from a transition to a blended learning solution. We've included several examples of common classroom training programs in this section of the book, along with the steps taken to convert them to a blended program.

These designs were created as examples of how blended learning programs can evolve. Because any effective training program should be designed to address your specific learning and business needs, these are not intended to be used as is, but rather are intended to provide you with practical illustrations.

Your final blended learning program design should stem from your needs assessment, consideration of feasible training solutions, and the design and development work that you have completed. Note that in each of the samples we've indicated that you should verify your original needs assessment and goals and objectives. We recommend that you avoid selecting training solutions simply because they are familiar (it's so easy to do), and instead consider all of the factors to determine what will be most effective for your situation.

For each of the six examples in this section, we start with the original needs assessment findings, followed by the original training program. Then we show how the steps to implement a blended learning program can be used to convert an existing program to a blended solution. The final page of each example is a sample of what a new blended program might look like.

Business Writing Training Program

Needs Assessment Key Findings

- Medium-sized telecommunications company

- Five hundred employees, all in one location

- Operations run during regular business hours

- Training room available (conference room)

- Literate, motivated workforce

- Content to be covered: Business-writing skills with a focus on increasing communication between various departments.

Original Training Program

Included full day, classroom-only session.

Agenda

Getting Started

- Overview
- Writing from the reader's perspective
- Writing for a diverse audience
- Keeping the end in mind
- Organizing your thoughts

Making Your Message Easy to Read

- Beginnings
- Endings
- Using headings
- Using bullets and lists

Creating Paragraphs and Sentences

- Topic sentences
- Sentence length
- Paragraph length

Using Terminology/Language

- Lingo
- Active/passive verbs
- Choosing first-person, second-person, third-person tense

Special Situations

- Netiquette
- Executive summaries
- Memos for all staff
- Sales letter
- Disciplinary letters

Constructing a Blended Learning Solution

Determine (Verify) the Need. When converting from traditional training to blended learning, verify that the needs assessment findings are still valid. The findings from the original needs assessment are listed above. The situation that prompted the needs assessment in the first place was that the company had grown quickly during the past year and found itself suffering from growing pains, one of which was a lack of communication between departments. Due to time constraints, employees found themselves using e-mail and other written reports to communicate rather than talking in person. Unfortunately, many of the newly hired employees were ineffective writers, and misunderstandings often resulted in poor decisions being made and rework being required, all of which cost the company money.

Create (Verify) Goals and Objectives. Verify that original learning goals and objectives are still valid.

Design the Blended Program. *Key factors:* A training room was available, as was a local business writing trainer. Mentors were available since the company had provided a similar training program several years earlier.

Create the design document: Since the employees were all in the same location, classroom training was selected as an effective way to provide information and practice activities and to introduce the participants to their mentors. Since the employees were generally self-motivated, job aids were selected to introduce some content and as a way to provide ongoing support once the employees were back on the job. Post-class writing assignments with the mentors helped to ensure a transfer of learning back to the job.

New Blended Learning Program

Includes job aids, classroom, and e-mail solutions.

Topic and Duration/Timing	Key Points	Training Solutions
Introductory Information (Job aids sent one week prior to the classroom session)	Making Your Message Easy to Read • Beginnings • Endings • Using headings • Using bullets and lists Using Terminology/Language • Lingo • Active/passive verbs • First person, second person, third person Special Situations • Netiquette • Executive summaries • Memos for all staff • Sales letter • Disciplinary letters	Job aids
Writing Basics (Three hours)	Getting Started • Overview • Writing from the reader's perspective • Writing for a diverse audience	Classroom session

Topic and Duration/Timing	Key Points	Training Solutions
	• Keeping the end in mind • Organizing your thoughts • Creating paragraphs and sentences • Topic sentences • Sentence length • Paragraph length Next Steps • Ongoing writing assignments • Mentor program	
Writing Practice (Following the classroom for eight consecutive weeks)	Post-class writing assignments are sent out each week by the program administrator, to be completed and reviewed with the mentor	Mentoring program E-mail

Customer Service Training Program

Needs Assessment Key Findings

- Regional retail establishment with twelve stores

- Five hundred employees, in three states

- Open seven days a week, with retail hours that adjust to seasons

- Numerous part-time employees on a variety of shifts

- Conference rooms available for training in each of the major stores

- Literate workforce well trained on sales transactions

- Employees mildly resistant to training

- Computer access available to all associates

- Content to be covered: customer service skills, both in person and on the telephone, for sales associates in all of the stores

Original Training Program

Included three days of classroom-only training.

Day One

Background of program and key principles
What is good customer service?
Why focus on customer service?

- The financial impact of service

- Repeat business

Lunch
Who are our customers?

- Internal and external customers

What do our customers expect from us?
Focusing and prioritizing the top expectations of customers

Day Two

Building rapport/how to communicate with customers
Attitude

- How to signal a friendly "ready to help" attitude that makes customers feel important

- How to effectively use voice inflection and body language to further communicate a positive message

What words and phrases help customers trust and like you?
Personality styles
Understanding styles
Typing ourselves and others

Lunch

How to make certain you deliver service that exceeds their expectations

Listening skills

- Three styles of listening

- Removing obstacles to listening

- Practicing proactive listening habits

Day Three

Telephone techniques

- Standing out from the competition

- Doing the basics better: greetings, holds, transfers, returning calls, and voicemail

Handling problems and complaints

- Recognizing the root sources of most misunderstandings and customer conflicts

- How to repair a damaged customer relationship

- How to say "no" when you have to without arousing resentment

Lunch

Dealing with difficult customers

- How to deal with unhappy, irrational, angry, and upset customers

- What to do when you feel yourself becoming angry with a customer

Wrap-up

Constructing a Blended Learning Solution

Determine (Verify) the Need. When converting from traditional training to blended learning, verify that the needs assessment findings are still valid. The original needs assessment was based on the following information: Customer service surveys are conducted on an ongoing basis. Feedback from the last quarter's survey indicates that customer satisfaction has dipped. Specific feedback indicates that store employees are not helpful to customers either in person or on the telephone. In addition, managers have observed employees not dealing with difficult customers in a productive manner. Of the store's five hundred employees, 350 of them provide direct service to the customer.

Create (Verify) Goals and Objectives. Verify that original learning goals and objectives are still valid.

Design the Blended Program. *Key factors:* The large number of employees and the subject matter (need for practice and feedback) affected the decision to select classroom training as one feasible solution. The various locations of employees and the variety of hours worked, combined with the availability of SMEs (managers) led to determining that self-study e-learning, on-the-job training, and job aids were also plausible.

Create the design document: As indicated above, the training content and other factors provided a large list of training solution options. While there was a desire to minimize classroom training time because it involved travel and overtime expenses, due to the subject matter and the slight resistance to the training, some classroom time was appropriate. The availability of SMEs (managers) provided the opportunity for conducting some of the training during staff meetings, which would also help to reduce the resistance, minimize classroom time, and aid in the transfer of learning from the classroom to the job.

New Blended Learning Program

Includes self-study and instructor-led pre-work, 1¾ days of classroom sessions, on-the-job practice, job aids, and an assessment instrument.

Topic and Duration/Timing	Key Points	Training Solutions
Pre-Work		
Customer service survey results (Three weeks prior to class)		E-mail with attached reading
The Customer **Isn't** Always Right (Two weeks prior to class)	• Video: *The Customer Isn't Always Right*	Video—available in their store's conference room
Classroom—Full Day		Classroom
Recap of survey results	• Serious issue	Read/discuss
Customer expectations	• What and why	Lecture
How to build rapport	• Skills and awareness	Demonstration/role play
Listening skills	• Three styles/when to use	Lecture/practice
Skill application assignment	• Build rapport and listen	OJT practice with manager Observation/feedback for one week
Post-Work		
	• Participants are asked to complete worksheets for the on-the-job skills practice and bring them to the next class in two weeks.	Self-reflection worksheets
	• Each participant is sent a personality style inventory to complete and return electronically.	Assessment instrument
	• Each manager shows the video *The Telephone Doctor Is In* during the weekly staff meeting and facilitates a discussion on the key points.	Classroom, discussion

(continued)

Topic and Duration/Timing	Key Points	Training Solutions
Classroom—¾ day		Classroom
Review skill application	• Lessons learned	Discussion
Personality style	• Yours and customers	Lecture/discussion
Telephone techniques	• Review video points	Discussion/role play
Difficult customers	• Four techniques to use	Lecture/practice and job aid
Post-Class		
	• Employees are sent an electronic examination to test their skill level following the class.	TBT, assessment
	• Employees are sent an e-mail reminder to access their job aids for reminders on techniques to use when dealing with difficult employees.	E-mail

Orientation Training Program

Needs Assessment Key Findings

- Manufacturing organization, headquartered in Minnesota

- Twelve hundred employees in three locations, all in Minnesota

- Operations run seven days a week, over three different shifts

- Classroom is available

- Training professional is available

- Computer training room is available

- Computer skills are limited

- Content to be covered: Welcome new employees to the organization, explain corporate culture and expectations, educate on corporate policies and procedures, conduct mandatory safety and ethics training, explain benefits, and collect completed benefits forms.

Original Training Program

Included classroom-only training (two days).

Morning of First Day

Welcome by the president and introduction to corporate culture

Corporate overview—organization charts, locations of facilities, vision, mission, and values

First half of policies and procedures manual

Lunch with your department

Afternoon of First Day

Second half of policies and procedures manual

Benefits explained

Morning of Second Day

Benefits forms signed and submitted

Corporate ethics video

Lunch

Afternoon of Second Day

Computer and phone usage

Mandatory safety training

Sign compliance forms

Constructing a Blended Learning Solution

Determine (Verify) the Need. When converting from traditional training to blended learning, verify that the needs assessment findings are still valid. The findings from the original needs assessment are listed here. A new employee orientation was needed by this organization due to legal and organization effectiveness reasons. Content for the training was determined by legal compliance, as well as the human resources department.

Create (Verify) Goals and Objectives. Verify that original learning goals and objectives are still valid.

Design the Blended Program. *Key factors:* Classroom and instructor availability, large number of participants, desire of senior management to have all the new employees meet headquarters staff and tour the facility, various shifts, and the capacity to deliver some of the content back on the job site.

Create the design document: Classroom, instructor availability, the numbers of participants and senior management's desire to have new employees meet headquarters staff and tour the facility all made classroom instruction a logical choice for the core portion of the program. Because some new employees had to travel to corporate headquarters for the orientation, the classroom time was limited to one day. Therefore, the content that was best delivered in person (due to the availability of a professional instructor or the need to interact with corporate staff) was all positioned on the first day of orientation and conducted in the classroom. Pre-work was sent out with an invitation to the orientation. On-the-job training was conducted immediately following the classroom session and was introduced during the corporate orientation, which helped connect all components of the program. The various shifts and the capability to deliver some of the content back on the job site were factors in selecting other training solutions that could occur on the job.

New Blended Learning Program

Includes pre-work, classroom, and OJT.

Topic and Duration/Timing	Key Points	Training Solutions
Prior to starting work	• Welcome letter • Benefits packet • Welcome video by president explaining corporate culture	Sent to the new employee at his or her home along with an invitation to the orientation session
Introductory Information and HR Forms (Full-day classroom)	• Corporate overview: organization charts, locations of facilities, vision, mission, and values • Policies manual distributed for employee review • Benefits forms signed and collected • Lunch and tour of headquarters • Overview of policies (distributed earlier) and questions answered • Mandatory safety training	Classroom session
Technology, Culture, and Expectations (Full-day OJT)	• Mentor trains on computer and phone usage • View corporate ethics video • Meet with manager to learn about performance expectations • Sign compliance forms	OJT

Software Implementation Training Program

Needs Assessment Key Findings

- Large medical technology company

- Approximately four thousand employees worldwide with seven manufacturing and engineering sites

- Primarily regular business hours, in seven different time zones

- Some of the staff are highly computer savvy; others rarely use a computer

- Technical infrastructure exists at each site, with employee-available workstations in lunch and break rooms

- Conference rooms are available at each site that will be converted temporarily into computer training rooms

- Technical trainers are available at each site

- Content to be covered: The company has decided to implement an online employee human resource information system that would allow employees to see their pay stubs and paid time off (PTO) accruals, make changes to their personal information, and access an enterprise-wide intranet, with customized content for their specific work sites.

Original Training Program

Included classroom-only sessions directed at different audiences.

Session 1

Introduction to Computers (audience: non-computer-literate employees)

- Basic Windows components
- Using a mouse
- Navigating
- Opening and closing programs

Session 2

Introduction to "Employee HR" (audience: all employees)

- Accessing your pay and PTO records
- Updating your personal HR information
- Navigating the new customized intranet

Session 3

Employee HR Super-Users (audience: selected "go-to" people at each site)

- Submitting pay and PTO requests
- Updating intranet information

Constructing a Blended Learning Solution

Determine (Verify) the Need. When converting from traditional training to blended learning, verify that the needs assessment findings are still valid. The findings from the original needs assessment demonstrated that a large number of potential users of the new online system were not computer literate, while another large group was computer literate and contained generally self-directed learners. The non-computer-literate employees clearly needed basic computer skills.

Create (Verify) Goals and Objectives. Verify that original learning goals and objectives are still valid.

Design the Blended Program. *Key factors:* Computer training classrooms and instructors were available, a wide variety of abilities and a large number of employees existed, employees were scattered in a variety of geographies and time zones.

Create the design document: Since many of the computer illiterate employees were apprehensive of computers in general, classroom training was chosen to provide hands-on, personalized training. Also, since technical trainers and a technical infrastructure were already in place and new computers had already been ordered to provide access to the new system for the manufacturing employees, setting up a temporary computer classroom in a conference room was a logical choice. The self-directed, computer-savvy learners were provided with TBTs that they could access at their convenience. Job aids were provided in two formats: online for the experienced computer users and paper copies for those new to computers. Open labs were scheduled where employees could practice and have a super-user/trainer available to answer questions. A mentoring program was set up to provide the super-users access to the technical trainers for additional information and support during the first six weeks following the implementation of "Employee HR."

New Blended Learning Program

Includes classroom, TBTs, job aids, webinars, and mentoring.

Topic and Duration/Timing	Key Points	Training Solutions
Introduction to Computers Audience: non-computer-literate employees Classroom: two-hour session	• Basic Windows components • Using a mouse • Navigating • Opening and closing programs	Classroom
Introduction to Employee HR Audience: all employees Classroom: two-hour session Job aids: distributed via e-mail and/or in classroom Open labs: scheduled two weeks after classroom/TBT distribution	• Accessing your pay and PTO records • Updating your personal HR information • Navigating the new customized intranet	Classroom for computer-illiterate employees, TBTs for others Scheduled open labs where employees could practice and have a super-user/trainer available to answer questions Job aids (online and paper formats)
Advanced Employee HR Audience: super-users Webinar: one-hour session Mentoring: post-webinar Job aids: referenced during webinar	• Submitting pay and PTO requests • Updating intranet information	Webinars Mentoring program (technical trainers matched with super-users) Job aids

Train-the-Trainer Program

Needs Assessment Key Findings

- Large university medical center with two hospitals and more than fifty clinics

- Twenty supervisors who will go through a train-the-trainer class and who will be expected to provide initial and ongoing training for the new scheduling system the medical center is implementing

- Two hundred employees who do the scheduling of clinical appointments and surgical operations

- Operations run seven days a week, over three different shifts (at the hospital sites)

- Classroom is available

- Training professional is available

- The staff are fairly computer literate

- Content to be covered: Two hundred employees must be trained on a new computer software program, so twenty supervisors are being trained to deliver the training to the other employees. This training program is designed to be a working session with two primary goals: (1) to edit the prepared training methods and materials to develop situation-specific training for each site and (2) to learn and practice effective delivery skills.

Original Training Program

Included three-day classroom-only sessions.

Day One

Opening activities

- Icebreaker

- Agenda and expectations

- Adult learning principles

- ADDIE model

Needs assessment

- Information to gather

- Analyze the components

- Wrap-up and preview

Day Two

Design your training session

- Write a training goal

- Write specific objectives

- Research and organize content information

- Determine training methods

- Design training materials

Develop your training session

- Build the training method components

- Produce the training materials

- Wrap-up and preview

Day Three

Facilitation skills

- Build rapport with the learners

- Observe and react

- Listen carefully

- Ask effective questions

Closing activities

- Next steps

- Summary of content

- Evaluation

Constructing a Blended Learning Solution

Determine (Verify) the Need. When converting from traditional training to blended learning, verify that the needs assessment findings are still valid. The original needs assessment stated that a new scheduling system was going to be implemented across the entire organization, creating a need for super-users and end-users at each site.

Create (Verify) Goals and Objectives. Verify that original learning goals and objectives are still valid.

Design the Blended Program. *Key factors:* The large number of employees who had to be trained, the availability of supervisors, the variety of shift workers, the computer competence of the employees, classroom and instructor availability, the interpersonal nature of the facilitation skills content.

Create the design document: The large number of employees who had to be trained and the availability of supervisors were influences in deciding to conduct a train-the-trainer session with the SMEs. The variety of shift workers and the computer competence of the employees were factors in the selection of conference calls, TBTs, and intranet sessions for the majority of the training program. Classroom and instructor availability, as well as the interpersonal nature of facilitation skills, made classroom instruction a logical choice for the facilitation portion of the program. Since much of the pre-work has to be completed by the participants about their individual situations, it was introduced in instructor-led webinars and conference call sessions and then sent out in two formats: (1) forms to be completed and (2) previously prepared materials that have to be edited to meet the specific needs of each site (for example, activities had to be changed to include situation-specific scenarios). Some of the content lent itself well to self-study, so was incorporated into self-study TBTs and simply introduced in instructor-led sessions.

New Blended Learning Program

Includes webinars, e-mail, teleconferences, and classroom sessions.

Topic and Duration/Timing	Key Points	Training Solutions
Introduction to TTT (One month prior to classroom session)	• Introductions • Agenda and Expectations • Adult Learning Principles Introduction (detailed TBTs to follow) • ADDIE Model Introduction (detailed TBTs to follow)	Instructor-led webinar
Basics of TTT (Sent following initial webinar session)	• Adult Learning Principles (link to online TBT) • ADDIE (link to online TBT)	TBT
Needs Assessment (Three weeks prior to classroom)	• Q&A from Adult Learning Principles and ADDIE content (follow-up) • Needs assessment • Information to gather overview (form to be sent/completed) • Analyze the components overview (form to be sent/completed) • Wrap-up and expectations for follow-up items	Instructor-led webinar
Needs Assessment (Following second webinar)	• Form to be completed: Information to Gather • Form to be completed: Components to Analyze	E-mail post-work
Goals and Objectives and Training Materials (Two weeks prior)	• Q&A from needs assessment forms • Write a training goal overview (form to be sent/completed)	Instructor-led webinar

(continued)

Topic and Duration/Timing	Key Points	Training Solutions
	• Write specific objectives overview (form to be sent/completed) • Research and organize content information • Training methods overview • Design/develop training materials (forms to be sent/completed)	
Goals and Objectives and Training Materials (Following third webinar)	• Form to be completed: Training Goals and Objectives • Materials to be edited: Sample Training Materials	E-mail post-work
Review Goals and Objectives and Training Materials (One week prior)	• Q&A from training goals and objectives • Review and questions from training materials • Wrap-up and preview	Conference call
Facilitation Skills	• Build rapport with the learners • Observe and react • Listen carefully • Ask effective questions	Classroom training session
Bringing It All Together	• Review of training agendas, methods, and materials • Evaluation	Classroom training session
Preparation for End-User Training (One week after the classroom session)	• Questions from classroom session • Questions in preparation of the end-user training	Conference call discussion
Evaluation Results (One week after the end-user training)	• Discussion of evaluation results	Conference call discussion

Management Training Program

Needs Assessment Key Findings

- Public sector, county government agency for large metropolitan area

- Forty-five employees in leadership roles to include supervisors, managers, and directors

- All located in the same building complex and all working the same shift

- Education and experience levels vary greatly

- Classroom and instructor available

- Computer-literate audience

- Content to be covered: County policies, employment law, all aspects of employee supervision (establishing expectations through managing performance), all aspects of operating a department (goal setting, budgeting, and others).

Original Training Program

Included three-day classroom management training session (total time: twenty-four hours).

Day One

Morning

Welcome and overview of leadership training program	President
Overview of county's expectations of all leaders	Trainer
County policies	Human Resources
Lunch	

Afternoon

Leader's responsibilities in upholding policies	Trainer
Employment law—FMLA, ADA, others	Legal staff

Day Two

Morning

Managing employees	Trainer
Setting performance expectations	
Providing feedback	
Taking corrective action	
Lunch	

Afternoon

Performance review system	Human Resources
Salary/compensation program	

Day Three

Morning

Recruiting and hiring of new employees	Human Resources
How to establish department goals	Trainer
Project/resource management	Trainer
Lunch	

Afternoon

Budgeting	Finance Department
Planning for professional development	Career development
Closing comments	President

Constructing a Blended Learning Solution

Determine (Verify) the Need. When converting from traditional training to blended learning, verify that the needs assessment findings are still valid. The original needs assessment was conducted using feedback from an employee opinion survey, which indicated that managers should develop leadership skills and increase knowledge of organizational policies and procedures.

Create (Verify) Goals and Objectives. Verify that original learning goals and objectives are still valid.

Design the Blended Program. *Key factors:* Availability of trainers and classroom; difficulty in having all of the managers away from their desks for days in a row; previous experience showed individual development needs existed among the managers and that the knowledge imparted in class was not always effectively transferred from the classroom to the job.

Create the design document: With all of the managers working the same shift and in the same location, a classroom solution appeared to be most practical.

However, to cover the content in the classroom would require three days of training, and having all managers away from work was impractical. A 360-degree feedback instrument was added to the training program to introduce the county's expectations of leaders as well as to address the issue of individual development needs. Along with coaching, this allowed for some individualized training for each manager on his or her own development needs. Using a technology-based training program to cover performance management allowed the managers to learn those materials at a time convenient for them, and it lessened the time they were away from their desks. Because of the availability of trainers and the classroom, classroom training remained the core of this program.

New Blended Learning Program

Includes 360-degree feedback instruments, coaching, TBTs, classroom, and pre-classroom reading.

Topic and Duration/Timing	Key Points	Training Solutions
Pre-work (360-degree feedback instruments distributed three weeks prior) Book sent two weeks prior	• All participants are asked to distribute 360-degree feedback instruments to their bosses, peers, and subordinates. • A book on leadership is sent to all participants for reading two weeks prior to first class.	• 360-degree feedback instruments • Reading assignment
Classroom—First Session	• Introduction and overview of county's expectations of all leaders and elements of the leadership training program • Introduction to county policies: demonstration, and practice locating them on the knowledge database • Distribution and interpretation of 360-degree feedback results	• Presentation • Demonstration • Hands-on practice • Discussion and self-reflection • Lunch discussion • Exercise: development plans • Interactivity • TBTs

Topic and Duration/Timing	Key Points	Training Solutions
	• Lunch with the executive team • Creation of development plans as a result of 360-degree feedback • Introduction of coaches (will work with participants on development activities) • Homework assignments: Complete TBT on performance management (setting expectations, giving feedback, and conducting performance reviews), look up performance review procedures, and locate forms on knowledge database, meet with coach once a week	• Coaching
Classroom— **Second Session** (Four weeks after first session)	• Review performance management steps/discuss questions • Role playing: giving performance feedback • Recruiting and hiring of new employees • How to establish department goals • Project/resource management • Homework: Use knowledge database to study budgeting process/forms and the career development resources; continue to meet once a week with coach	• Discussion • Role playing • Presentation • Hands-on practice • Coaching
Graduation Lunch (Four weeks after second session)	• Meet with other participants and coaches • Brief review of materials, discussion of questions or issues, and celebration of completion of program	• Group discussion

INDEX

A

Adult learning principles: and program design, 51–52; summary of, 104; teaching of, 105; used in classroom training, 92

Assessment instruments, 113–123; as alternative learning method, 121; and analysis of results, 119; bias and, 119; blended with classroom training, 121–122; common types of, 115; confidentiality and, 119; credibility of, 118; defined, 44; evaluation process and, 122; examples of, 128–131, 241–273; implementation of, 116–120; and literacy level of respondent, 118; multi-rater, 115, 118; and needs analysis, 116–117, 121; pros and cons of using, 115–116; resources for, 123–125; selection considerations, 117–119; and test anxiety, 122; as training solution, 114–122; usefulness and effectiveness of, 116

B

Blended learning: advantages of, 13–16; definitions of, 3, 12; and diverse learner needs, 15–16; promotion of, 72; traditional classroom training in, 12

Blended Learning: The Here and Now, 13

Blended program design, 43–53; adult learning principles and, 51–52; common pitfalls in, 20–21; and coordination of training solutions, 59–60; and course content, 49–50; creating design document for, 50–51; decision matrix for, 50, 54–55, 58; determining scope of, 20; project manager's role in, 71; and real-life examples, 52; six-step process in, 17–20; and training options, 43–46

Blended program goals, 18–19; determination of, 33–34; examples of, 37–38; learning objectives and, 35; statement of, 33

Blended program implementation: basic elements of, 69–70; and business needs,

ABOUT THE AUTHORS

Diann Wilson is the training and organization development manager for the San Diego County Regional Airport Authority in San Diego, California. She is an experienced training and development professional with over twenty years of experience in the fields of education, training, and organization effectiveness. Wilson has developed and delivered dynamic training seminars (using a variety of training solutions) on a wide variety of topics, including management skills, goal setting, meeting facilitation skills, and performance management. She has her master's degree in training and organization development from the University of Minnesota and has work experience in the fields of education, healthcare, government, and manufacturing. As an active member in local professional associations, she has been a speaker at both ASTD and Organization Development Network chapter meetings.

Ellen Smilanich is the owner of Smilanich Consulting, Ltd., in Minneapolis, Minnesota, and has over eighteen years of experience in training, human resources, and personal and career coaching. Smilanich (pronounced "smile an itch") has delivered training seminars locally, nationally, and internationally on a variety of topics, including facilitation and presentation skills, team building, career development, and proprietary software programs. She holds a master's degree in human resource development with an emphasis in training and development and has worked in the fields of healthcare, education, and software.

Pfeiffer Publications Guide

This guide is designed to familiarize you with the various types of Pfeiffer publications. The formats section describes the various types of products that we publish; the methodologies section describes the many different ways that content might be provided within a product. We also provide a list of the topic areas in which we publish.

FORMATS

In addition to its extensive book-publishing program, Pfeiffer offers content in an array of formats, from fieldbooks for the practitioner to complete, ready-to-use training packages that support group learning.

FIELDBOOK Designed to provide information and guidance to practitioners in the midst of action. Most fieldbooks are companions to another, sometimes earlier, work, from which its ideas are derived; the fieldbook makes practical what was theoretical in the original text. Fieldbooks can certainly be read from cover to cover. More likely, though, you'll find yourself bouncing around following a particular theme, or dipping in as the mood, and the situation, dictate.

HANDBOOK A contributed volume of work on a single topic, comprising an eclectic mix of ideas, case studies, and best practices sourced by practitioners and experts in the field.

An editor or team of editors usually is appointed to seek out contributors and to evaluate content for relevance to the topic. Think of a handbook not as a ready-to-eat meal, but as a cookbook of ingredients that enables you to create the most fitting experience for the occasion.

RESOURCE Materials designed to support group learning. They come in many forms: a complete, ready-to-use exercise (such as a game); a comprehensive resource on one topic (such as conflict management) containing a variety of methods and approaches; or a collection of like-minded activities (such as icebreakers) on multiple subjects and situations.

TRAINING PACKAGE An entire, ready-to-use learning program that focuses on a particular topic or skill. All packages comprise a guide for the facilitator/trainer and a workbook for the participants. Some packages are supported with additional media—such as video—or learning aids, instruments, or other devices to help participants understand concepts or practice and develop skills.

- *Facilitator/trainer's guide* Contains an introduction to the program, advice on how to organize and facilitate the learning event, and step-by-step instructor notes. The guide also contains copies of presentation materials—handouts, presentations, and overhead designs, for example—used in the program.

- *Participant's workbook* Contains exercises and reading materials that support the learning goal and serves as a valuable reference and support guide for participants in the weeks and months that follow the learning event. Typically, each participant will require his or her own workbook.

ELECTRONIC CD-ROMs and Web-based products transform static Pfeiffer content into dynamic, interactive experiences. Designed to take advantage of the searchability, automation, and ease-of-use that technology provides, our e-products bring convenience and immediate accessibility to your workspace.

METHODOLOGIES

CASE STUDY A presentation, in narrative form, of an actual event that has occurred inside an organization. Case studies are not prescriptive, nor are they used to prove a point; they are designed to develop critical analysis and decision-making skills. A case study has a specific time frame, specifies a sequence of events, is narrative in structure, and contains a plot structure—an issue (what should be/have been done?). Use case studies when the goal is to enable participants to apply previously learned theories to the circumstances in the case, decide what is pertinent, identify the real issues, decide what should have been done, and develop a plan of action.

ENERGIZER A short activity that develops readiness for the next session or learning event. Energizers are most commonly used after a break or lunch to stimulate or refocus the group. Many involve some form of physical activity, so they are a useful way to counter post-lunch lethargy. Other uses include transitioning from one topic to another, where "mental" distancing is important.

EXPERIENTIAL LEARNING ACTIVITY (ELA) A facilitator-led intervention that moves participants through the learning cycle from experience to application (also known as a Structured Experience). ELAs are carefully thought-out designs in which there is a definite learning purpose and intended outcome. Each step—everything that participants do during the activity—facilitates the accomplishment of the stated goal. Each ELA includes complete instructions for facilitating the intervention and a clear statement of goals, suggested group size and timing, materials required, an explanation of the process, and, where appropriate, possible variations to the activity. (For more detail on Experiential Learning Activities, see the Introduction to the *Reference Guide to Handbooks and Annuals*, 1999 edition, Pfeiffer, San Francisco.)

GAME A group activity that has the purpose of fostering team spirit and togetherness in addition to the achievement of a pre-stated goal. Usually contrived—undertaking a desert expedition, for example—this type of learning method offers an engaging means for participants to demonstrate and practice business and interpersonal skills. Games are effective for team building and personal development mainly because the goal is subordinate to the process—the means through which participants reach decisions, collaborate, communicate, and generate trust and understanding. Games often engage teams in "friendly" competition.

ICEBREAKER A (usually) short activity designed to help participants overcome initial anxiety in a training session and/or to acquaint the participants with one another. An icebreaker can be a fun activity or can be tied to specific topics or training goals. While a useful tool in itself, the icebreaker comes into its own in situations where tension or resistance exists within a group.

INSTRUMENT A device used to assess, appraise, evaluate, describe, classify, and summarize various aspects of human behavior. The term used to describe an instrument depends primarily on its format and purpose. These terms include survey, questionnaire, inventory, diagnostic, survey, and poll. Some uses of instruments include providing instrumental feedback to group members, studying here-and-now processes or functioning within a group, manipulating group composition, and evaluating outcomes of training and other interventions.

Instruments are popular in the training and HR field because, in general, more growth can occur if an individual is provided with a method for focusing specifically on his or her own behavior. Instruments also are used to obtain information that will serve as a basis for change and to assist in workforce planning efforts.

Paper-and-pencil tests still dominate the instrument landscape with a typical package comprising a facilitator's guide, which offers advice on administering the instrument and interpreting the collected data, and an initial set of instruments. Additional instruments are available separately. Pfeiffer, though, is investing heavily in e-instruments. Electronic instrumentation provides effortless distribution and, for larger groups particularly, offers advantages over paper-and-pencil tests in the time it takes to analyze data and provide feedback.

LECTURETTE A short talk that provides an explanation of a principle, model, or process that is pertinent to the participants' current learning needs. A lecturette is intended to establish a common language bond between the trainer and the participants by providing a mutual frame of reference. Use a lecturette as an introduction to a group activity or event, as an interjection during an event, or as a handout.

MODEL A graphic depiction of a system or process and the relationship among its elements. Models provide a frame of reference and something more tangible, and more easily remembered, than a verbal explanation. They also give participants something to "go on," enabling them to track their own progress as they experience the dynamics, processes, and relationships being depicted in the model.

ROLE PLAY A technique in which people assume a role in a situation/scenario: a customer service rep in an angry-customer exchange, for example. The way in which the role is approached is then discussed and feedback is offered. The role play is often repeated using a different approach and/or incorporating changes made based on feedback received. In other words, role playing is a spontaneous interaction involving realistic behavior under artificial (and safe) conditions.

SIMULATION A methodology for understanding the interrelationships among components of a system or process. Simulations differ from games in that they test or use a model that depicts or mirrors some aspect of reality in form, if not necessarily in content. Learning occurs by studying the effects of change on one or more factors of the model. Simulations are commonly used to test hypotheses about what happens in a system—often referred to as "what if?" analysis—or to examine best-case/worst-case scenarios.

THEORY A presentation of an idea from a conjectural perspective. Theories are useful because they encourage us to examine behavior and phenomena through a different lens.

TOPICS

The twin goals of providing effective and practical solutions for workforce training and organization development and meeting the educational needs of training and human resource professionals shape Pfeiffer's publishing program. Core topics include the following:

Leadership & Management

Communication & Presentation

Coaching & Mentoring

Training & Development

e-Learning

Teams & Collaboration

OD & Strategic Planning

Human Resources

Consulting